T0271725

"In his new book on the 12 a~~nimals~~
Zhongxian has given us an auth~~entic~~
ancient Chinese system of astrology, which in Chinese ~~tradition goes~~
hand-and-glove with the Yijing ('Book of Change'). And since Wu's
previous book revealed the essence of the Yijing, we now have the
whole story on Chinese astrology and divination, clear as a bell. I
highly recommend this book to all serious students and readers in the
field of classical Chinese culture."

—*Daniel Reid, author of* The Tao of Health, Sex &
Longevity *and* My Journey in Mystic China

"Master Wu's new book is most accessible to those who are interested
in acquiring this ancient Chinese wisdom. His widely acknowledged
lineage from various schools of Qigong, martial and philosophical
traditions serves him well in this very special, handsomely produced
little gem of a book. I highly recommend it!"

—*Chungliang Al Huang, founder-president, Living Tao
Foundation and author of* Embrace Tiger, Return to
Mountain *and* The Chinese Book of Animal Powers

"Master Zhongxian Wu has made a complex Eastern topic accessible
to the Western reader. Far beyond other sources, this book helps you
understand your destiny as described by the 12 animal symbols of
Yijing wisdom, helping you reach your personal potential. It helps you
accurately determine your yearly, monthly, and even hourly animal
symbol, and explains how each can affect your health, relationship,
career, and finances. Master Wu writes 'Life is Magic'…and this book
helps you understand it."

—*Steve Rhodes, editor of* Qi: The Journal of Traditional
Eastern Health and Medicine (Qi Journal)

"In our secret Kabbalah teachings we deal with 12 permutations of the
divine name governing the year. I find that when I also look at Master
Wu's 12 gates that I understand our own tradition so much better. I
recommend his book wholeheartedly."

—*Rabbi Zalman Schachter-Shalomi,
co-author of* Jewish With Feeling

THE
12
Chinese
Animals

by the same author

Seeking the Spirit of The Book of Change
8 Days to Mastering a Shamanic Yijing (I Ching) Prediction System
Foreword by Daniel Reid
ISBN 978 1 84819 020 7

THE
12
Chinese
Animals

*Create Harmony in your
Daily Life through
Ancient Chinese Wisdom*

Master Zhongxian Wu

SINGING DRAGON
LONDON AND PHILADELPHIA

First edition published in hardback in Great Britain in 2010 by
Singing Dragon, an imprint of Jessica Kingsley Publishers

This paperback edition published in Great Britain in 2021 by Singing Dragon,
an imprint of Jessica Kingsley Publishers
An Hachette Company

6

A CIP catalogue record for this title is available from the British Library and
the Library of Congress

ISBN 978 1 78775 765 3
eISBN 978 0 85701 015 5

Printed and bound by CPI Group (UK) Ltd, Croydon, CR0 4YY

Jessica Kingsley Publishers' policy is to use papers that are natural, renewable
and recyclable products and made from wood grown in sustainable forests.
The logging and manufacturing processes are expected to conform to the
environmental regulations of the country of origin.

Jessica Kingsley Publishers
73 Collier Street
London N1 9BE, UK

www.singingdragon.com

To my precious wife
Karin Elizabeth Taylor Wu

Contents

Acknowledgments

This book is the fruit of loving support from family, friends, and nature.

Nature is the greatest inspiration for my writings. I have visited many magical places throughout China, the United Kingdom, and North America, and find that nature is always guiding me to live a harmonious life. I am grateful for all the enchanted places I have been – with each breath, I feel the nature spirits with me, uplifting my spirit on a daily basis. I especially appreciate the small, cozy home in the foothills of the Blue Ridge Mountains of Virginia, which was made available for me to write this book.

I want to acknowledge Jessica Kingsley for asking me to write this book after seeing my calligraphy in May 2009, and her Singing Dragon imprint for bringing this book to us.

Many thanks to Helena Ström Taylor for her artistic eye in photographing my cultivation postures, and for her skillfulness in making my calligraphy accessible for the book.

Special thanks to my dear wife, Karin Elizabeth Taylor Wu, for her expert editing and for her gentle spirit of love, care, and support in our daily life together.

Zhongxian Wu
December 2009

Introduction

THE
WISDOM
OF 12

L iving in harmony within family, among society, and with nature is the ancient Chinese way of life. People in China have enjoyed living in a harmonious society for thousands of years, at least since the time of the Western Zhou Dynasty (1122 to 771 BCE). In Chinese, we have an expression to illustrate this style of life, *ye bu bi hu, lu bu shi yi* (夜不閉戶, 路不拾遺): there is no need to close your door at night, and no one will pick up your belongings (if dropped) on the road — an assurance that society at large is honorable. In ancient China, there were no religions, no police, no taxes, and no lawyers. There was only a special kind of wisdom to guide Chinese people to cultivate their true humanity. This true humanity contains the spirit of love, compassion, faith, courtesy, justice, and humbleness. With this true humanity, people are able to respect each other, support each other, and create a harmonious community together.

You might be wondering about this wisdom. This wisdom is still held in some ancient Chinese classics; *Yijing* 易經 (*I Ching, The Book of Change*) is one of them. *Yijing* wisdom has guided countless Chinese to live in harmony in their daily lives for thousands of years. One of the most important concepts in the Chinese wisdom traditions is trinity; three in one, is one. *Yijing* contains three secret and sacred layers of wisdom: semiotics (the study of signs and symbols and their use or interpretation), numerology, and philosophy. This book will give you a taste of this ancient Chinese wisdom. By understanding the 12 animal symbols and 12 tidal hexagrams from *Yijing* wisdom, you will be able to learn a way to find your inner peace and live in harmony with your family, your community, and with nature.

The wisdom of *Yijing* is vast; it looks like a tree of the universe. The roots of the tree embrace the entire earth and the tips of the tree hold the entire heavenly realm. There is a tiny branch on this tree, called the 12 animal symbols system, which is related to your birth, your energetic life cycle or destiny, 12 tidal hexagrams of *Yijing*, and the cycle of nature. It is also a small sub-branch of the *Yijing* prediction system. As I emphasized in the Afterword of my book *Seeking the Spirit of The Book of Change: 8 Days to Mastering a Shamanic Yijing (I Ching) Prediction System*, *Yijing* prediction is magic, but it is also an art, a way of life, a way of nature, and it is a way of the Universe. It is a way to express the great universal compassion, which gives birth to all beings and protects them.[*] The spirit of *Yijing* prediction is to help people find a way to change their lives and experience living in a consistently peaceful state, especially during difficult situations. This prediction system provides a way for people to live in harmony.

Life is magic! The 12 animal symbols of *Yijing* wisdom are a way to help you to understand this magic, and to help you live a harmonious life. In this book, I will share with you how these 12 animal symbols can help you understand your destiny. Using the wisdom of the animal symbols as guides, you will be better able to appreciate your personality, to make choices that positively influence your health, relationships, career, and finances, and to know which colors and foods are most beneficial, so that you can live up to your greatest potential. It will be easier for you

---

[*]   Wu, Zhongxian. *Seeking the Spirit of The Book of Change: 8 Days to Mastering a Shamanic Yijing (I Ching) Prediction System*. London: Singing Dragon. 2009: 213.

to apply the wisdom of the 12 animal symbols in your life if I provide you with some fundamentals about the number 12, Chinese astrology and animal symbols, and the Eight Trigrams and 12 tidal hexagrams of *Yijing*. Let's discuss some of this information before we start our journey through the 12 animal symbols.

I. NUMEROLOGICAL MEANINGS OF 12

While you are likely familiar with the 12 hour clock, you may be less so with the idea of the Universal Clock. By Chinese shamanic definition, the Universe is the union of time and space. Time is specifically defined as past, present, and future, while space is described as above, below, front, back, left, and right. The Universal Clock is an ancient Chinese concept of the 12 energetic patterns, or stages, of all natural cycles. Each pattern of 12 within the Universal Clock represents both time *and* space. For example, if you imagine the 12 o'clock position on an analog clock, you may only have an associated sense of time. However, by the Universal Clock, this 12 o'clock position also designates a positional sense – *above*, or the top position. Additionally, the 12 o'clock position describes the time and space of a life cycle. For example, 12 o'clock can represent middle age or the peak of life. The Universal Clock is a way of expressing the natural rhythm of time and space in the universe.

In ancient times, people lived closer to the cycles of nature and followed the way of nature. This harmonious lifestyle is patterned in a Chinese phrase, *ri chu er zuo, ri luo er xi* 日出而作, 日落而息 (sunrise, go to work; sunset, go to rest), which depicts a simple way of life that follows the pattern of the sun. Through their observation of nature, ancient Chinese understood that each natural cycle (i.e. daily, monthly, annually, and the cycle of life itself) have 12 different stages. The number 12 was an important aspect of daily life.

In Chinese, the number 12 is represented by the character *Shier* 十二, which is also a symbol for the Universal Clock. In Chinese cosmology, the number 12 represents the energetic and physiological changes our bodies experience in the 12 *Chen* 辰 per day (one *Chen* is a two hour segment), the 12 months of a year, and the 12 years of a life cycle. In Chinese medicine, the number 12 also corresponds to the 12 organs and meridian systems in the human body. The human body itself is seen as a microcosmic representation of the macrocosm of the Universe. Ancient Chinese shamans used the 12 tidal hexagrams of *Yijing* to describe the 12 energetic patterns of the microcosm (the human body) and the macrocosm (nature and the Universe).

II. CHINESE ASTROLOGY AND 12 ANIMAL SYMBOLS

Are you familiar with Chinese astrology? You may think of the 12 animals of the Chinese zodiac commonly printed on restaurant menus. In actuality, Chinese astrology is vastly more complex than this.

Chinese Astrology is based on ancient Chinese cosmology and the Five Elements theory. Each individualized astrological chart is a life reading that uses these elements to give insight into a person's past, present, and future. Having your chart read by a skilled practitioner will give you precise guidance about health, career, relationships, and more.

An individual Chinese astrology chart is constructed by determining the Heavenly Stem and Earthly Branch for each year, month, day, and hour of birth. What does this mean? There are ten Heavenly Stems in Chinese astrology, which reflect how the Heavenly Way (for example, stars, planets and weather patterns) affects the human body. The 12 Earthly Branches in this system represent the waxing and waning of all natural cycles. The understanding of Heavenly Stems and Earthly Branches comes from thousands of years of observing astronomical phenomena, and is quite possibly older than the invention of the Chinese characters, of which the oldest recorded evidence dates back 8000 years.* Numerous examples of the symbols for the Heavenly Stems and Earthly Branches are seen in the unearthed ancient Chinese oracle bones from the Shang 商 Dynasty (1766 to 1111 BCE).

The name for Chinese astrology is *BaZi* 八字 (eight characters). This is because the entire chart is composed of eight characters – one Heavenly Stem and one Earthly Branch for each year, month, day, and hour of birth. Each pair is known as One Pillar. Together, the chart has Four Pillars, *SiZhu* 四柱 in Chinese.

As you can see, for any particular individual, there will be eight characters (*BaZi*) that reflect the personal energies derived from all the Heavenly Stems and Earthly Branches within the Four Pillars that support the body. In other words, by understanding the energy of the macrocosmic Universe at the exact birth time, we can understand the microcosm of the individual. This is because in Chinese shamanism, in the spiritual level, there is no separation between past, present, and future. If you truly understand the patterns of the past, you directly see their influence on patterns of the present and in the future.

In Chinese tradition, we commonly use the 12 animal symbols to represent the 12 Earthly Branches in the astrological

---

*   Wu, Zhongxian. *Vital Breath of the Dao – Chinese Shamanic Tiger Qigong.* St. Paul, MN: Dragon Door. 2006: 10.

chart. It is easier for people to use the symbolic meaning of the animals to understand their life patterns. These 12 animal symbols are Rat, Ox, Tiger, Rabbit, Dragon, Snake, Horse, Goat, Monkey, Rooster, Dog, and Pig. In "The Beginning" of this book, I will introduce the way to find your fundamental power animal symbols (see p.27). You will then be able to learn the wisdom of your personal animals in subsequent chapters. Knowing the exact conditions of the universe when you were born will help you actualize your greatest potential now and in the future. This awareness will direct you to find your inner peace, which will allow you to live more harmoniously with your family and friends, your community, and with nature.

III. EIGHT TRIGRAMS, 12 TIDAL HEXAGRAMS, AND THE CYCLE OF NATURE

There are 12 very important hexagrams in the *Yijing* system, the 12 tidal hexagrams. These hexagrams represent the energetic patterns of their related animal symbol in Chinese astrology. We use the wisdom contained within these tidal hexagrams to give guidance during an astrology consultation. The *Yijing* system is the basis of all astrology consultations. The entire *Yijing* text is made of 64 hexagrams. Each hexagram was created by joining two trigrams. When the two become one, a new symbol is generated. Having an appreciation of each trigram will help you deepen your knowledge of each hexagram, and thus, of the entire *Yijing* system. Let me share some information about the trigrams before we further discuss the 12 tidal hexagrams.

According to the *Yijing*, *Bagua*, or the Eight Trigrams, is the model of the Universe. Everything in existence, including every part of the body, can be classified by one of the trigrams. Ancient shamans understood this connection and brought it into their divinations.* Trigrams are symbols made up of three lines, representing Heaven, Earth, and the Human Being. Three lines become one symbol, and this symbol now contains three secret and sacred layers of wisdom. Each trigram reflects an essential aspect of the Universe. The Eight Trigrams are: *Qian* 乾 (Heaven), *Dui* 兌 (Marsh or Lake), *Li* 離 (Fire), *Zhen* 震 (Thunder), *Xun* 巽 (Wind), *Kan* 坎 (Water), *Gen* 艮 (Mountain), and *Kun* 坤 (Earth). The lines that make up each trigram will be either a solid line (–) or a broken line (--). The solid line is called the *Yang* 陽 line and the broken line is called the *Yin* 陰 line. I will cite some of the symbolic meanings of the Eight Trigrams from Chapter 4 of my book *Seeking the Spirit of The Book of Change* here for your convenience.**

In *Yijing*, we use three unbroken lines to represent the image of sky, and this is the trigram of *Qian*. The original meaning of *Qian* is the rising *Qi* or energy. The ascending *Qi* formed Heaven, according to ancient Chinese cosmology, so the trigram *Qian* represents Heaven. By Heaven we do not simply mean Heaven or sky, but all functions of the Universe, including the movements of the planets and stars. The movement of the cosmos is absolutely there, in constant motion. This is the energetic meaning of *Qian*. The three unbroken lines of *Qian* are the image of the quality of the sky. We could use the trigram *Qian* to represent anything that has that strong uplifting spirit or energetic quality. *Qian* is anything that draws upward and perseveres, just like the planets in the sky keep their rotation, and never stop running.

---

* Wu, Zhongxian. *Seeking the Spirit of The Book of Change: 8 Days to Mastering a Shamanic Yijing (I Ching) Prediction System*. London: Singing Dragon. 2009: 67.

** Wu, Zhongxian. *Seeking the Spirit of The Book of Change: 8 Days to Mastering a Shamanic Yijing (I Ching) Prediction System*. London: Singing Dragon. 2009: 99–120.

We use the trigram with one broken line on top and two solid lines at the bottom to represent the energetic quality of *Dui* (Lake). The Chinese character for *Dui* means communication, negotiation, and any kind of exchange. Ancient Chinese shamans considered a lake or marsh to be an open mouth of the Earth that communicates with Heaven. If you spend time observing a marsh, you notice that the marsh itself is always changing, and that it supports an abundance of life. Like the marsh, *Dui* is also a symbol of change and transformation, and the joy of life itself.

The trigram *Li* (Fire) has one *Yin* line between two *Yang* lines. The original meaning of the Chinese character *Li* is the name for a bird with colorful feathers. It symbolizes anything that is colorful and bright. In Chinese shamanic traditions, a bird represents the spirit, and is the spiritual animal of the Heart. Therefore, the trigram *Li* (Fire) also represents your spirit and your heart.

The trigram *Zhen* (Thunder) has one solid line at the bottom and two broken lines on top. The Chinese character *Zhen* means shake, vibrate, or move. Thunder represents this quality of shaking, the vibration of the world shaking. From the perspective of ancient Chinese shamanism, the roaring of thunder is the spirit of nature, waking up all beings. *Zhen* is used to describe something that shakes new-life energy into any situation.

The trigram *Xun* (Wind) has one broken line at the bottom and two solid lines on the top. The Chinese character *Xun* means magnificent or prepared and is the symbol for the harmonious winds of spring, which bring nature into full bloom and prosperity. *Xun* is a symbol for vitality and life energy, and it has strong momentum. The attribute of *Xun* is the ability to proceed and to propagate in a gentle manner. It manifests *Qi*, breath, romantic love, news, order, and discipline.

THE WISDOM OF 12

The trigram *Kan* (Water) has one unbroken line between two broken lines. The Chinese character *Kan* means entrapment, trap, danger, collapse, or difficult. The trigram *Kan* also shows us the hardness or strong power hidden under a surface of weakness or softness. Water is the presenter of this trigram. Water contains a dangerous quality, like a hidden trap. For example, deep water, rivers, lakes, and oceans may look peaceful and quiet on the surface, but this can be deceiving. Water represents the mystery and the unknown. Chinese shamans believe that Water is the most mystical element, the first element born from the Universe. Life began in water. It holds such significance in Chinese medicine, that water is used as the most important medicine in the healing process.

The trigram *Gen* (Mountain) has one unbroken line on top and two broken lines at the bottom. This trigram looks like an overturned bowl and gives us a very stable feeling. The Chinese character *Gen* means stop, hold, or stability. A mountain represents the stability and spiritual quality of the trigram *Gen*. It indicates that in our daily life, we need to have internal stability, just like a mountain.

The trigram *Kun* (Earth) has three broken lines, representing the Earth quality of openness, greatness, and carrying everything. Like the mother, the Earth holds everything. The Chinese character *Kun* 坤 is made by the left radical *Tu* 土, which means Earth element, and the right radical *Shen* 申, which means stretch, lightning, or spirit. *Kun* stands for the nature spirits that are hidden within the Earth. Earth does not show off, yet it holds, carries, and supports all beings.

Now, let us take a look at the 12 tidal hexagrams, which are used to depict the energetic cycles of nature. In Chinese, we call these hexagrams *Shier Xiaoxi Gua* 十二消息卦. *Shier* means 12, while *Xiao* means decrease, reduce, waning, and *Xi* means increase, gain, waxing; together, *Xiaoxi* means information, the waxing and waning of the tides, or the changing faces of the moon. *Gua* means trigram or hexagram. In general, we translate *Shier Xiaoxi Gua* as 12 tidal hexagrams.

These 12 tidal hexagrams depict different energetic stages of the cycles of nature or of life patterns. They help us to understand the 12 month annual cycle of nature, learn the 12 meridian systems of the body, and make sense of the 12 different stages of life. The 12 tidal hexagrams are: *Fu* 復 (Rebirth), *Lin* 臨 (Deliver), *Tai* 泰 (Balance), *DaZhuang* 大壯 (Prosper), *Guai* 夬 (Transform), *Qian* 乾 (Strengthen), *Gou* 姤 (Copulate), *Dun* 遯 (Retreat), *Pi* 否 (Break), *Guan* 觀 (Observe), *Bo* 剝 (Peel), and *Kun* 坤 (Flow). These 12 also reflect the continuous cycle of energy change, for example, the rhythm of day turning into night, or the change of seasons.

You can look at the 12 hexagrams together and see that they form a pattern of steadily increasing, then decreasing intensity (see "Wave Figure of 12 Tidal Hexagrams" on p.25). This is the natural wave pattern of life.

The hexagrams *Fu* 復 (Rebirth), *Lin* 臨 (Deliver), *Tai* 泰 (Balance), *DaZhuang* 大壯 (Prosper), *Guai* 夬 (Transform), and *Qian* 乾 (Strengthen) represent the six waxing stages of the rising *Yang* energy pattern, until *Yang* reaches its peak.

The hexagrams *Gou* 姤 (Copulate), *Dun* 遯 (Retreat), *Pi* 否 (Break), *Guan* 觀 (Observe), *Bo* 剝 (Peel), and *Kun* 坤 (Flow) illustrate the *Yang* energy dropping to its nadir and *Yin* energy rising to its zenith in the six stages of the declining *Yang* energy pattern.

Together, these 12 tidal hexagrams symbolize a perfect wave of life. I am sure that all of us have experienced times of great joy and times of sorrow. No one could live in their climax of life all the time. The *Yijing* wisdom of these 12 tidal hexagrams gives us great guidance to live harmoniously through different life stages. We will discuss some details of the hexagrams as they relate to their associated animal symbol later in this book. Traditionally, these 12 hexagrams are also used to describe your energy state during specific internal cultivation practices like meditation, Qigong, and Taiji. I will share different internal cultivation methods connected with the 12 tidal hexagrams at the end of each chapter in the book. I hope you will be able to use the practices to better understand the wisdom of the 12 animal symbols and the 12 tidal hexagrams, and to strengthen your life force and find your inner peace.

Table 1 illustrates the aforementioned correspondences.

Table 1. The 12 Stages of the Life Cycle

Number Order	Earthly Branch	Animal	Hexagram	Chen/Time	Meridian
1	Zi 子	Rat	Fu 復 (Rebirth)	23:00 – 00:59	Gallbladder
2	Chou 丑	Ox	Lin 臨 (Deliver)	01:00 – 02:59	Liver
3	Yin 寅	Tiger	Tai 泰 (Balance)	03:00 – 04:59	Lung
4	Mao 卯	Rabbit	DaZhuang 大壯 (Prosper)	05:00 – 06:59	Large intestine
5	Chen 辰	Dragon	Guai 夬 (Transform)	07:00 – 08:59	Stomach
6	Si 巳	Snake	Qian 乾 (Strengthen)	09:00 – 10:59	Spleen
7	Wu 午	Horse	Gou 姤 (Copulate)	11:00 – 12:59	Heart
8	Wei 未	Goat	Dun 遯 (Retreat)	13:00 – 14:59	Small intestine
9	Shen 申	Monkey	Pi 否 (Break)	15:00 – 16:59	Bladder
10	You 酉	Rooster	Guan 觀 (Observe)	17:00 – 18:59	Kidney
11	Xu 戌	Dog	Bo 剝 (Peel)	19:00 – 20:59	Pericardium
12	Hai 亥	Pig	Kun 坤 (Flow)	21:00 – 22:59	Triple burner

蓮化全乎心　宇宙立於手

The Universe is within my hand
and is manifested through my heart.

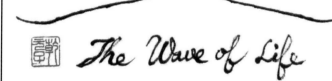

坤　剝　觀　否　遯　姤　乾　夬　大壯　泰　臨　復

Kun　Bo　Guan　Pi　Dun　Gou　Qian　Guai　DaZhuang　Tai　Lin　Fu

The Wave of Life

Wave Figure of 12 Tidal Hexagrams

The Beginning

FINDING
YOUR
ANIMALS

In the West, most information available to the public on how to find your Chinese animal symbol is incomplete and misleading. Many Chinese animal sign or horoscope books and popular websites will tell you that each animal symbol starts from the Chinese New Year in the Chinese Lunar calendar. This is, in fact, an incorrect method to find your animal symbol.

Generally speaking when most people talk about Chinese animal symbols, they are referring to the yearly animal symbol. For instance, if you were born in 1951, most readily available resources will tell you that your animal symbol is Rabbit, based on the assumption that 1951 is the Year of Rabbit in the Chinese zodiac system. Actually, being born in 1951 does not always mean you will have Rabbit as your animal symbol. Furthermore, according to Chinese astrology, you have at least four animal symbols in your birth chart! The yearly animal symbol is related to the energetic year in which you were born, the monthly animal symbol is related to the energetic month in which you were born, the daily animal symbol is related to the energetic day on which you were born, and the hourly animal symbol is related to the energetic hour in which you were born. I emphasize the energetic year, month, day, and hour because they are different concepts than those of the regular solar calendar.

Let us discuss some brief information about the Chinese calendar before I introduce the way to find your animal symbols.

It will help us better understand the way of finding your animals.

Many people think that the Chinese calendar is a lunar calendar. In fact, the Chinese calendar is not a lunar calendar; it is a kind of lunisolar calendar which we call *WanNianLi* 萬年曆 or *YinYangLi* 陰陽歷 in Chinese. *WanNianLi* translates as "ten thousand years calendar" and *YinYangLi* means moon and sun calendar. *Yin* corresponds to the moon, *Yang* stands for the sun, and *Li* means calendar. In the *YinYangLi*, the date points out both the moon phase and the time of the solar year. We use 24 *JieQi* 節氣 to determine the sun position and the time of a solar year. In Chinese cosmology, we divide one year into 24 *JieQi*, which means that each *JieQi* is a period of time lasting approximately 15 days. In English, we commonly translate *JieQi* as Solar Term or Segment; the 24 *JieQi* symbolize the 24 sun positions in the sky and the 24 energetic patterns of a year. In particular, the 24 *JieQi* are formed by 12 *Jie* 節 and 12 *Qi* 氣. *Jie* means rhythm, segment, or section, and is used to indicate the starting of an energetic month. *Qi* means energy, breath, or pulse, and specifies the middle point of the energetic month. In Chinese astrology, we have to apply *Jie*, the beginning of the energetic month, to identify properly in which *Jie* the energetic month and the energetic year begin, so that we can determine the correct animal symbols.

As I mentioned earlier, you have at least four animal symbols in your birth chart. We will discuss how to find three of these four – your energetic yearly, monthly, and hourly animal symbols. In Chinese tradition, we use 12 Earthly Branches to represent the 12 energetic years, 12 energetic months, and 12 energetic hours. These cycles of 12 are easy to follow – most of us can keep track of the two 12 hour cycles in a day and the 12 months that make up a year, and, if it was necessary, you could add or subtract 12 years from a given starting point. Although we also use the 12 Earthly Branches to represent the 12 energetic days, the daily animal symbols are more complicated to figure out. This is because it is much more challenging to keep track of 12 day cycles. The Chinese calendar began approximately 4709 years ago. In order to determine the animal symbol for the day you were born, we would have to count in 12 day cycles, starting from the first day of the Chinese calendar, 4709 years ago, until the day you were born! It is, of course, possible to use a traditional Chinese calendar book to find this information out more quickly. Unfortunately, as far as I know, there are no English versions of these books available. This book is not about the Chinese calendar and I do not feel it is a good idea to translate the entire calendar book here. I hope now you can better understand why I will focus on helping you find your animal symbols for your energetic year, month and hour. Let us start with finding your yearly animal symbol.

Yearly Animal Symbol

LiChun 立春 is the marker for an energetic year animal symbol. *LiChun* means the beginning of the spring season, and it is one of the 12 *Jie* in the 24 *JieQi* system. In particular, it refers to the moment when the sun is exactly at the celestial longitude of 315°. It usually occurs on February 4 or 5 each year in the Gregorian solar calendar. An energetic animal symbol year begins with the *LiChun* in its present year till the following *LiChun*. For instance, *LiChun* in 2008 was on February 4, 2008 at 19:00, and in 2009, it was on February 4, 2009 at 00:49. When we say 2008 is the Year of Rat, it is really accurate to say that the Rat Year of 2008 begins on February 4, 2008 at 19:00 (*LiChun 2008*) and ends on February 4, 2009 at 00:48 (please remember that *LiChun 2008* began at 00:49). If a girl was born on February 4, 2008 at 18:59, what is her Chinese animal symbol? Rat? Not at all. She is not a Rat symbol person because her time of birth was before the *LiChun* in 2008. Instead, her animal symbol is the 2007 energetic yearly animal, which is Pig.

If you want to know your own or someone else's yearly animal symbol, first check when the starting of the spring season, the *LiChun*, is in the birth year. If the birth time is before the *LiChun* in that year, the animal symbol is actually the previous energetic year's animal symbol; if the birth time is after the *LiChun*, the animal symbol is the present energetic yearly animal symbol. Let us take a look at more examples. Assume you were born on January 28, 1973 at 19:21. First, you check the *LiChun* in 1973 and see that it was February 4, 1973 at 07:04. Because your birth time was before the *LiChun*, your animal symbol is not the 1973 yearly animal Ox, it is the 1972 yearly animal symbol Rat. If you were born on March 15, 1973 at 16:02, your animal symbol would be Ox because your birthday is after the *LiChun*.

Table 2 is a yearly animal symbol index table with the *LiChun* at the Gregorian solar calendar time (see p.34). I made this chart so you can easily find the *LiChun* time for the year in which you were born. From the first row, find the year in which you were born – the years are organized in ten year increments. For example, if you were born in 1950, find the *LiChun* time of 1950 by looking down the column marked 1948–1959. If you were born at, or after, 17:20 on February 4, you can see that your associated Earthly Branch is *Yin* and animal symbol is Tiger. If instead you were born at, or before, 17:19 on February 4, you can see that your associated Earthly Branch is *Chou* and animal symbol is Ox. Please go ahead and find your yearly animal symbol now.

Monthly Animal Symbol

The way to find your monthly animal symbol is similar to the way you found your yearly animal symbol. Just as before, we will not use the lunar month or the Gregorian solar calendar month, but the energetic month. The energetic month depends on the *JieQi* system, and we count them from one *Jie* to the following *Jie*. For instance, the monthly animal Rat begins at a time we call *DaXue* 大雪, and ends at a time known as *XiaoHan* 小寒. *DaXue* means major snow or great snow. It is one of the *Jie* (15 day segments) in the 24 *JieQi* of the year. It specifically refers to the moment when the sun is exactly at the celestial longitude of 255°. When referring to the Gregorian solar calendar, it usually falls on December 7 each year. *XiaoHan* means minor cold or small cold, and it is the *Jie* immediately following *DaXue*. *XiaoHan* begins the moment the sun is exactly at the celestial longitude of 285°. By the Gregorian solar calendar, it usually occurs on January 5 each year. Therefore, the Rat monthly animal symbol is generally between December 7 and January 5. If your birthday falls within two days of December 7 or January 5, the very beginning or end of the Rat month, please check the exact time for *DaXue* or *XiaoHan* in the Chinese calendar book or ask someone who can read Chinese characters to help you. You will need to make sure that your birthday is after the *Jie* for the associated animal symbol, because the time of each *Jie* is different every year. Let us look at some examples.

DaXue in 1977 was on December 7, 1977 at 13:30. If your birthday was December 7, 1977 at 13:29, then your monthly animal symbol was not Rat because your birth time was before the *DaXue*. Instead, your animal symbol is that of the previous energetic month, which is Pig. If your birthday was on December 7, 1977 at 13:30, your animal symbol is Rat. The following *Jie*, *XiaoHan*, was on January 6, 1978 at 00:43. Your

Table 2. Yearly Animal Symbols Index

Order	1924 – 1935	1936 – 1947	1948 – 1959	1960 – 1971	1972 – 1983	1984 – 1995	1996 – 2007	2008 – 2019	Earthly Branch	Animal Symbol
1	Feb. 5 1924 09:49	Feb. 5 1936 07:29	Feb. 5 1948 05:41	Feb. 5 1960 03:23	Feb. 5 1972 01:20	Feb 4 1984 23:18	Feb. 4 1996 21:07	Feb. 4 2008 19:00	*Zi* 子	Rat
2	Feb. 4 1925 15:36	Feb. 4 1937 13:25	Feb. 4 1949 11:22	Feb. 4 1961 09:22	Feb. 4 1973 07:04	Feb 4 1985 05:11	Feb. 4 1997 03:01	Feb. 4 2009 00:49	*Chou* 丑	Ox
3	Feb. 4 1926 21:38	Feb. 4 1938 19:14	Feb. 4 1950 17:20	Feb. 4 1962 15:17	Feb. 4 1974 13:00	Feb 4 1986 11:07	Feb. 4 1998 08:56	Feb. 4 2010 06:47	*Yin* 寅	Tiger
4	Feb. 5 1927 03:30	Feb. 5 1939 01:10	Feb. 4 1951 23:13	Feb. 4 1963 21:07	Feb. 4 1975 18:59	Feb. 4 1987 16:51	Feb. 4 1999 14:57	Feb. 4 2011 12:32	*Mao* 卯	Rabbit
5	Feb. 5 1928 09:16	Feb. 5 1940 07:07	Feb. 5 1952 04:52	Feb. 5 1964 03:04	Feb. 5 1976 00:39	Feb 4 1988 22:42	Feb. 4 2000 20:40	Feb. 4 2012 18:22	*Chen* 辰	Dragon

#	Animal								
6	*Si* 巳 Snake	Feb. 4 1929 15:08	Feb. 4 1941 12:49	Feb. 4 1953 10:45	Feb. 4 1965 08:46	Feb. 4 1977 06:33	Feb. 4 1989 04:27	Feb. 4 2001 02:28	Feb. 4 2013 00:13
7	*Wu* 午 Horse	Feb. 4 1930 20:51	Feb. 4 1942 18:48	Feb. 4 1954 16:30	Feb. 4 1966 14:37	Feb. 4 1978 12:26	Feb. 4 1990 10:14	Feb. 4 2002 08:24	Feb. 4 2014 06:03
8	*Wei* 未 Goat	Feb. 5 1931 02:40	Feb. 5 1943 00:40	Feb. 4 1955 22:17	Feb. 4 1967 20:30	Feb. 4 1979 18:12	Feb. 4 1991 16:08	Feb. 4 2003 14:05	Feb. 4 2015 11:58
9	*Shen* 申 Monkey	Feb. 5 1932 08:29	Feb. 5 1944 06:22	Feb. 5 1956 04:11	Feb. 5 1968 02:07	Feb. 5 1980 00:09	Feb. 4 1992 21:48	Feb. 4 2004 19:56	Feb. 4 2016 17:45
10	*You* 酉 Rooster	Feb. 4 1933 14:09	Feb. 4 1945 12:19	Feb. 4 1957 09:54	Feb. 4 1969 07:58	Feb. 4 1981 05:55	Feb. 4 1993 03:37	Feb. 4 2005 01:43	Feb. 3 2017 23:33
11	*Xu* 戌 Dog	Feb. 4 1934 20:03	Feb. 4 1946 18:03	Feb. 4 1958 15:49	Feb. 4 1970 13:45	Feb. 4 1982 11:45	Feb. 4 1994 09:30	Feb. 4 2006 07:27	Feb. 4 2018 05:28
12	*Hai* 亥 Pig	Feb. 5 1935 01:48	Feb. 4 1947 23:50	Feb. 4 1959 21:42	Feb. 4 1971 19:25	Feb. 4 1983 17:39	Feb. 4 1995 15:12	Feb. 4 2007 13:18	Feb. 4 2019 11:14

Table 3. Monthly Animal Symbols Index

Order	Jie	English Translation	Dates	Earthly Branch	Animal Symbol
1	DaXue 大雪	Major Snow	December 7	Zi 子	Rat
2	XiaoHan 小寒	Minor Cold	January 6	Chou 丑	Ox
3	LiChun 立春	Starting Spring	February 4	Yin 寅	Tiger
4	JingZhe 驚蟄	Awakening Hibernation	March 6	Mao 卯	Rabbit
5	QingMing 清明	Pure Brightness	April 5	Chen 辰	Dragon
6	LiXia 立夏	Starting Summer	May 6	Si 巳	Snake
7	MangZhong 芒種	Plumpy Grain	June 6	Wu 午	Horse
8	XiaoShu 小暑	Minor Heat	July 7	Wei 未	Goat
9	LiQiu 立秋	Starting Autumn	August 8	Shen 申	Monkey
10	BaiLu 白露	White Dew	September 8	You 酉	Rooster
11	HanLu 寒露	Cold Dew	October 8	Xu 戌	Dog
12	LiDong 立冬	Starting Winter	November 7	Hai 亥	Pig

monthly animal symbol is Rat if your birthday was January 6, 1978 at 00:42, and your animal symbol is the next monthly animal symbol, Ox, if your birthday is January 6, 1978 at 00:44.

I will convert the 12 *Jie* to the approximate dates in the Gregorian solar calendar, and tell you the associated monthly animal symbols. I hope this will make it convenient for you to determine your monthly animal symbol. As you can see in Table 3, Rat starts at *DaXue* (Major Snow), which usually falls on December 7. Please find the *Jie* for your energetic birth month by looking at Table 3. Again, I would like to emphasize that you will need to check the exact time of the *Jie* if your birthday falls within two days before or after the dates in Table 3.

Hourly Animal Symbol

Your hourly animal symbol is easy to figure out. Remember that one energetic hour, *Chen*, is equal to two hours in the 24 hour daily system. If, for example, your birth time was between 23:00 and 00:59, your hourly animal symbol is Rat. Please use Table 4 to find your hourly animal symbol.

In this book, in addition to giving you specific information related to your yearly, monthly, and hourly animal symbols, I will also share with you some general information about each animal symbol in its related chapter. You now know that you will be learning more about your own personal animal symbols, and may be feeling a little confused about which animal symbol is the most important in helping you live a more peaceful and harmonious life. First, carefully read about your monthly animal symbol – it is the most important animal symbol in your chart because it will give you the most information about the general destination of your life. Your monthly animal symbol provides

Table 4. Hourly Animal Symbols Index

Order	Time	Earthly Branch	Animal Symbol
1	23:00 – 00:59	Zi 子	Rat
2	01:00 – 02:59	Chou 丑	Ox
3	03:00 – 04:59	Yin 寅	Tiger
4	05:00 – 06:59	Mao 卯	Rabbit
5	07:00 – 08:59	Chen 辰	Dragon
6	09:00 – 10:59	Si 巳	Snake
7	11:00 – 12:59	Wu 午	Horse
8	13:00 – 14:59	Wei 未	Goat
9	15:00 – 16:59	Shen 申	Monkey
10	17:00 – 18:59	You 酉	Rooster
11	19:00 – 20:59	Xu 戌	Dog
12	21:00 – 22:59	Hai 亥	Pig

the best information about the most productive years of your life. Next, pay attention to your yearly animal symbol, as it will give you good insight into the early stages of your life. Finally, seek guidance from your hourly animal symbol to learn how to live up to your greatest potential in the later stages in your life.

I hope this book will help you to live in harmony.

Good luck!

Master Zhongxian Wu

The

ANIMALS

1

Rat and *Fu*
復 (Rebirth)

The rat is good at hiding in the darkness or in a hole, is most active at night, and is known for its strong ability to survive. Considering these natural characteristics, it may be easier for you to understand that the Rat is a symbol for wisdom and strong new life energy in Chinese tradition. It is the first animal symbol in the 12 Chinese Animals System. It is a time or a place where *Yang* or new life energy starts in a new life cycle, which we represent with the tidal hexagram *Fu*. We use *Zi* 子 to represent the Rat symbol in 12 Earthly Branches. Earthly Branches, you may remember from the introduction, represent the waxing and waning *Yin* and *Yang* throughout the 12 *Chen* (two hour segments) of a day and 12 months of a year. *Zi* is a symbol for midnight of each day and for the eleventh month in the Chinese Lunar-Solar calendar. In this calendar, the winter solstice falls in the middle of the eleventh month. As you can see, the Earthly Branch *Zi* represents both the beginning and end of a day or the beginning and end of a year.

Having a Rat animal symbol in your Chinese birth chart means you are smart, flexible, optimistic, and open minded. You have a great intuitive sense which helps you make decisions. This strong intuition explains why you have such a strong living ability – you are a survivor. No matter where you go, you have an easy time making new friends, and fit yourself readily into your new environment. People so enjoy your charming character that you often find yourself surrounded by people. It would be a wise choice if you have a creative job, like being a writer, musician, artist, inventor, or reformer. One warning to you: never overdepend on your great intuition; it is always good to deliberate your ideas before you make decisions based on your intuition alone. This is especially important when you start a new relationship – if you go around just spontaneously following your intuition, you will mess up your life!

If Rat is your yearly animal symbol, you will have an easy life when you are young. You can achieve your goals and have a successful business at an early age if you can be stable and commit yourself. A great opportunity may be wasted if you cannot be constant in your efforts.

If Rat is your monthly animal symbol, you have strong ambitions. You may have a weak body as a young person. Even though you are resourceful and can build a flourishing life by your own means, your honesty and trust will provide you with strong support from family and friends

If Rat is your hourly animal symbol, you have a strong personality, and it is important for you to cultivate the ability to consider other people's feelings. You are very flexible, and it can sometimes be difficult for you to be consistent if you are in the habit of constantly changing your mind. Be careful, this changeability can make your life feel unstable! Generally speaking, you do not have trouble making money. Take care of yourself and be sure to go on nice vacations when you are 36, 46, and 58 years old, which may be challenging years for you with regard to your health.

Rat Landscape (Rebirth, Return to the Light)

Breathing through
the dark period

White snow brings pure land

Thunder power hidden
within roots

Know the Light is returning

I will categorize some general Rat features here for your further interest.

Personality

You are flexible, optimistic, and open minded; you are flowing like water in the social river and easily find your own way of life. Your good intuition will help you make decisions about your future direction very quickly. As uncontrolled water can cause disastrous flooding, it is important for you to practice meditation techniques to control your intuitive mind.

Health

You do not have major health issues and will live a long life. A little thing you need to be careful about is your digestive function. When your digestion is troubled, it may also affect your kidney and heart function.

Relationships

A Monkey or Dragon person may be your soul mate, or at least your close friend. An Ox or Pig person can be a great business partner for you. Be aware of the Goat person because there are always some conflicts between you guys. Try to make peace with the Horse person because you both get into fights easily – sometimes for no real reason! You will have simple relationships with people who have the other animal symbols in their chart.

Career

With your creative ability, you can be a writer, musician, artist, inventor, reformer, or political leader very well. Being your own boss is always a smart choice.

Finance

Money will come to you if the purpose of your work is to help others with enthusiasm. You are likely to have good financial returns if you do so, and may have a more difficult time making money if you work only for money. In general, spring and summer are good seasons for you to make new financial plans.

Color

Black is your spiritual color – like it or not! The color black will help you feel deeply connected with your spirit. Green is the color to help you find your own potential energy and talent. You should wear green clothes when you have social activities, especially public speeches or lectures. Yellow or brown colors will help you feel grounded. Red is your financial color. Having some red in your office will bring you good luck with your finances. White is your spiritual source color: you should have it in your cultivation room or bedroom, which will nourish your body physically and spiritually.

Food

Root vegetables, black beans, pork, beef, and fish are good for you.

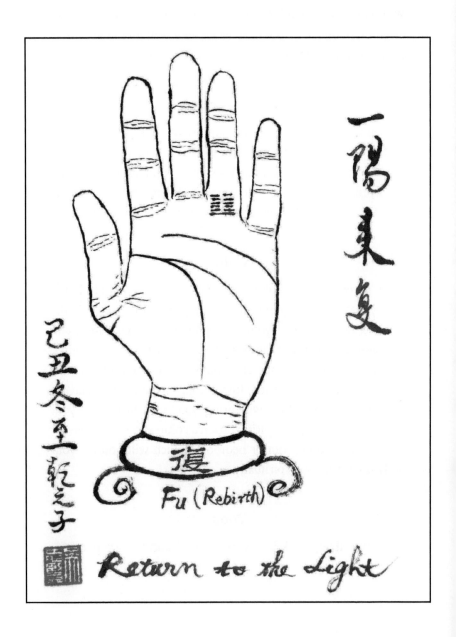

一陽來復

己丑冬至 乾元子

復
Fu (Rebirth)

Return to the Light

Fu (Rebirth)

Fu is the tidal hexagram that represents the energetic pattern of the Rat animal symbol. The Chinese character *Fu* means return, repeat, recover, and rebirth. The symbol of the hexagram is made with one *Yang* line at the bottom and five *Yin* lines on top, which represents *Yang Qi,* or new life energy, returning back in a natural cycle. It is the symbol for rebirth and rejuvenation.

In an annual cycle, *Fu* represents *Zi* – the month in which the winter solstice occurs. *Zi* lasts from approximately December 7 to January 5 in the solar calendar. The winter solstice is the shortest day and longest night of the year, which in Chinese tradition means that *Yang Qi* has dropped to its nadir and *Yin Qi* has climbed to its zenith. Literally, the winter solstice marks the point at which we begin to experience the gradual reversal of lengthening nights and shortening days. The winter solstice is the turning point of *Yang* energy. Depending on the sun's changing position, the winter solstice occurs some time between December 21 and December 22 each year (in the northern hemisphere).

In old Chinese tradition, we have a big winter solstice celebration. It was one of my favorite childhood festivals. In my memory, families gathered in the kitchen to prepare the sacrificial food on the winter solstice eve. My grandmother made many kinds of animal dolls from rice flour. My brother and I would help make the *TangYuan* (small rice balls). In the early morning of the next day, the first thing my family did was bring out rice animal dolls and *TangYuan* and other sacrificial foods to offer to nature. Although most modern city people in China do not make this kind of offering, most northern Chinese families still eat *JiaoZi* (dumplings) and most southern Chinese families still eat *TangYuan* at the winter solstice.

Both *JiaoZi* and *TangYuan* are symbols representing *Yang Qi*. Eating *JiaoZi* or *TangYuan* during the winter solstice is a way to remind us to hold *Yang* energy within and keep warm during the cold winter. In Chinese wisdom traditions, it is one of the best times of the year to do your inner cultivation because the universal *Yin* energy will reach the peak level and the *Yang* energy will be reborn. We need to spend more time doing Qigong and meditation to support the rebirth of our inner *Yang* energy on the winter solstice day.

In the daily cycle, *Fu* stands for *Zi* time, which is 23:00–00:59. Like the winter solstice, midnight is the time when *Yang Qi* regenerates in your body and begins to increase. *Zi* is a great time for you to do inner cultivation. Or, if you are not practicing any inner cultivation, it would be a good habit to go to bed before 23:00.

Let us uncover more information about *Fu* from *Yijing* wisdom. Like all hexagrams, the hexagram *Fu* is made up of two trigrams. In this hexagram, the top trigram is *Kun* (Earth) and the bottom trigram is *Zhen* (Thunder). It is an image of Thunder within the Earth. Thunder is the symbol for shaking off old patterns of stagnation and creating new life energy or power. Earth is the symbol for holding yourself stable or centering your mind. Hence, the hexagram *Fu* is an image of inner cultivation. Just like your meditation, when you steady your body, mind, and breath, you will be able to feel your *Yang Qi* generating automatically within your body. If you can center yourself from deep within, you may feel *Qi* shaking in your body just like thunder and lightning.

When I do not feel well or when I am beginning to feel sick, the first thing I do is to practice some Qigong or meditation to help me refine my life energy and recover by the inner cultivation. Many of my students have recovered from sickness through their Qigong or Taiji practice. When I have a challenge in my life, the first thing I do is to take a deep breath to my Dantian (the center and reservoir of our life energy, which is located in the lower belly) and bring my mind back to my body. And this always helps me shift the challenge quickly and makes my life easy and peaceful. This is what I have learned from the hexagram *Fu* (Rebirth). I hope you can try some inner cultivation with me at *Fu* time, the time that will give you a feeling of rebirth every day. I would be happy if you learned more about the hexagram *Fu* from your inner cultivation practice.

Inner Cultivation *Fu* ceremony

At 11pm every night, light a candle in front of you and start the meditation with your hands in the *Fu* mudra.

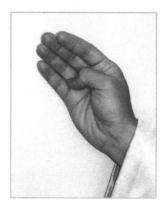

The *Fu* mudra is made by touching each thumb to the base of the ring fingers. The palmar crease of the ring finger is associated with the hexagram *Fu*. Make sure to keep your fingers together and relaxed. Then, place your mudra with palms on your belly and middle fingers touching the navel. First open your eyes and look directly at the candlelight. Then, close your eyes and imagine the candlelight in your Dantian. Adjust your breathing to be slow, smooth, deep, and even. Feel how each breath makes the light brighter and brighter in your Dantian. Meditate as long as you can. Before ending, please say a little prayer:

*"May the Spiritual Lights shine
within my heart and body,*

*May the Spiritual Lights shine within
my family and friends,*

May the Spiritual Lights shine within all beings,

*May the Spiritual Lights always shine with
peace and harmony for the World."*

2

Ox and *Lin*
臨 (Deliver)

三五牛臨說而順大亨以正

戊子冬吉日
亮元于首書

The ox has a close relationship with human beings. In early agricultural society, humans relied heavily on the ox for hard labor in the field. Oxen work slowly, and are prized for their strong power and their ability to work constantly for long periods of time. Ox is a symbol for endurance, fortitude, and stamina in Chinese tradition. It is the second animal symbol in the 12 Chinese Animals System. We use *Chou* 丑 to represent the Ox symbol in the 12 Earthly Branches. *Chou* is a symbol for the 01:00–02:59 time of day, and for the twelfth month in the Chinese Lunar-Solar calendar, which is approximately January 6 to February 4 in the Gregorian solar calendar. *Chou* represents the darkest time of day and the coldest month of the year. It is a time or a place where *Yang* energy (life energy) is working hard to deliver the next stage in a new life cycle. We use the tidal hexagram *Lin* to symbolize Ox.

Having an Ox animal symbol in your Chinese birth chart suggests you are gentle, stable, straight, vocal, and vital, and can sometimes be stubborn or obstinate. You have great endurance and stamina, which will help you achieve your goals. Oxen are ruminants, chewing, swallowing, and regurgitating the same food repeatedly. Just as oxen ruminate their food over and over, you have a tendency to ruminate your thoughts again and again before making decisions. This might give others the impression that you are a slow person. However, no matter how difficult the situation is, once your decision is made, your steady nature will allow you to complete your tasks.

People like your gentleness and patient character. Sometimes, you have a strong temper. You would do well to choose a stable job, such as a teacher, counselor, or doctor, or a government job. When you work directly with people, you would be wise to continually cultivate your flexibility; otherwise, you may come across as being arrogant or prejudiced. The most important thing for you to remember if you are in a relationship is to learn how to truly listen to your partner's voice and hear their needs.

If Ox is your yearly animal symbol, you will likely have a hard life when you are young – driven to challenge yourself and work very hard. However, you are able to achieve your goals and be successful in business because of your tough work, diligence, and enduring effort. You might feel very lonely sometimes, if you generally do not receive enough support from your parents and family.

If Ox is your monthly animal symbol, you have great compassion for others. You are very independent and can be a workaholic. You rarely take the opportunity to get together with your parents and siblings.

If Ox is your hourly animal symbol, you have a great life. People pay respect to you no matter what you are doing. You are in charge of what you are doing. Make sure to take good care of yourself and have nice vacations when you are 18, 26, 31, and 46 years old. During these potentially difficult years, it would be wise to adopt a vegetarian diet in order to avoid significant health challenges.

Ox Landscape (Deliver, Speak your Truth)

Mysterious lake beneath the Earth

Reflecting Dao, the
Heavenly Path

Darkest moment before the dawn

Standing firm, the challenge way

I will categorize some general Ox features here for your further interest.

Personality

You are gentle, stable, straight, vocal, and vital, and can sometimes be stubborn or obstinate. You are stable, like a mountain on the earth. You center yourself very well in almost every situation, even in very tough times. Your great patience, vigor, compassion, and meditative mind will help you complete your tasks and achieve your greatest goals in life. Like soil in the field, plants could not grow if the soil is heavy and dry; in order to flourish, learn to use your natural tendency to ruminate to cultivate a flexible attitude.

Health

You will live long if you experience minor illnesses once in a while throughout your life. Please take good care of yourself and have a good rest every day. Do not overwork! Otherwise, you will exhaust your liver, and your life force, and will end up suddenly clashing with yourself someday.

Relationships

A Snake or Rooster person may be your soul mate, or at least can be your very close friend. A Rat or Pig person will make a great business partner for you. Be careful around a Horse person because it is easy to have some conflicts between you two. Try to make peace with a Goat person – sometimes, you two get into fights for no real reason. You will have simple relationships with other animal symbol people.

Career

With your ruminating mind and fortitude, you can be well suited as a teacher, counselor, doctor, sales person, realtor, or government official.

Finance

You have a good ability to make money. You might become very rich when you are young through hard work. In general, winter and summer are good seasons for you to increase your financial power.

Color

Yellow or brown are your spirit's original colors, and will always help you feel deeply connected with your spirit. White is the color that will help you find your own potential energy and talent. You should wear white clothes when you have an important social activity, such as public speaking or lecturing. Green will help you feel grounded. As black is your financial color, it will bring you good luck in your finances to have some black in your office. Red is your spiritual source color, and having it in your cultivation room or bedroom will nourish your body physically and spiritually.

Food

Green vegetables, soybeans, fermented foods, beef, and fish are good for you.

Lin (Deliver)

Speak Your Truth

Lin (Deliver)

Lin is the tidal hexagram that represents the energetic pattern of the Ox animal symbol. The Chinese character *Lin* means look down from above, keep watch on, face, confront, arrive, govern, rule, and deliver. The symbol of the hexagram is made with two *Yang* lines on the bottom with four *Yin* lines on top. This symbol represents *Yang Qi*, or life energy, getting stronger than the previous pattern *Fu*, in a natural cycle. It is also a symbol meaning to recreate. The symbolic meaning of *Lin* is similar to a woman in labor, about to deliver her new baby. It represents the time or place where you can start your new life or new business, but must work very hard to do so.

In an annual cycle, *Lin* represents the *Chou* month, which occurs from approximately January 6 to February 4 in a solar calendar. This is the last month of the winter season according to Chinese cosmology. It is also the coldest time of year in the northern hemisphere. It is the most difficult season for animals to find food to survive. As you can imagine, when humans were living in an ancient agricultural society, this was the most difficult time of year for them to find food for survival as well. Like hibernation, when animals conserve energy because there are few resources available, *Chou* symbolizes preserving your energy during the most difficult time or situation. During the winter months, nature holds its energy within before bursting forth with spring. *Chou* also represents the wisdom of waiting for the right opportunity to show off your talents.

In a daily cycle, *Lin* stands for *Chou* time, which is 01:00–02:59. This time period is comparable to the last month in winter, when hibernating animals are deep in their hibernating state. This is the time that you need to be inactive and to be deep in slumber. It is the best sleeping time for you to recharge yourself.

Let us discover more information about *Lin* from *Yijing* wisdom. The hexagram *Lin* is made up of two trigrams: the top trigram is *Kun* (Earth) and the bottom trigram is *Dui* (Lake). It is an image of a Lake within the Earth. Lake is the symbol for changing old patterns and transformation into new life energy or power. Again, Earth is the symbol for holding yourself stable or centering your mind. The hexagram *Lin* is an image of a person with a stable and rooted mind, looking down from a high position, able to clearly see transformation occurring beneath the surface. *Lin* is also the image of you in meditation: steady your body, mind, and breath. In the mean time, bring your eyesight back to your body in order to look down to your lower belly. This will allow you to feel your *Yang Qi* delivering to your whole body effortlessly, providing ultimate nourishment.

The wisdom of the hexagram *Lin* (Deliver) advises us that we should be steady, constant, and never give up when we are experiencing a hard time. It also tells us that it is important to take our time to look within, holding our energy back while we wait for the opportunity for transformation. If you are feeling sick, use perspective to help you to see the situation clearly, so that you can find a best modality to help you recover. I hope you can try some inner cultivation with me at *Lin* time; it is a time for you to deliver your inner power and wisdom into your life.

Inner Cultivation *Lin* ceremony

At any time when you need help making a new decision, or during a difficult situation, light a candle in front of you and start this meditation.

First straighten your back and feel that your body is stable like a mountain. Then, make the *Lin* mudra by placing each thumb on the palmar crease of the middle finger. The palmar crease of the middle finger is related to the hexagram *Lin*. Keeping your fingers relaxed and close together, place your palms on your knees. Adjust your breathing to be slow, smooth, deep, and even. Feel each breath connecting with your spleen, kidney, and lung. Meditate as long as you can. Before ending, please say a little prayer:

"May the Spiritual Lights shine within my organs,
May the Spiritual Lights shine within my spirit,
May the Spiritual Lights guide me to live with serenity."

3

Tiger and *Tai*
泰 (Balance)

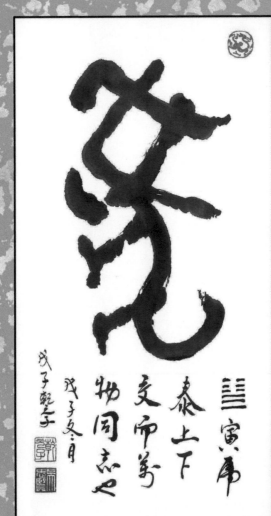

乾

䷊ 寅年

戊子輕之字

泰上下
交而萬
物同志也

戊子冬二月

The tiger has a wild nature and needs a big space or territory for living. Tigers act slowly and carefully while stalking their prey, and move very quickly and with great power once they start their attack. In the Chinese tradition, Tiger is a symbol for caution, valiance, power, optimism, attraction, and ambition. It is the third animal symbol in the 12 Chinese Animals System. We use Yin 寅 to represent the Tiger symbol in the 12 Earthly Branches. Yin is a symbol for the 03:00–04:59 time of day, and for the first month in the Chinese Lunar-Solar calendar, which is approximately February 4 to March 6 in the Gregorian solar calendar. Yin represents dawn in the daily cycle, and the first month of spring in the yearly cycle. It can represent either a time or a place in which Yang energy (life energy) is awakening its newest stage in a new life cycle. We use the tidal hexagram Tai to symbolize Tiger.

Having a Tiger animal symbol in your Chinese birth chart suggests that you are careful, graceful, powerful, enthusiastic, friendly, and attractive. It is also common for Tiger people to be easily angered, have difficulties taking advice, or have challenges with authority. As a Tiger animal person, you have great caution and vitality, which will help you to achieve your goals. You have a strong desire to get things done once you have a plan formulated. You would be wise to cultivate the ability to be calm and flexible. It will serve you to refine your tendency to be very direct when you communicate with others, so that when necessary, you are able to express yourself in a softer way. Doing so will help you reach your destination no matter how difficult the situation is.

Generally speaking, you have pretty good luck in life. People will gladly support your leadership if you know how to respect differing opinions. You would do well to choose an independent job, like being your own boss, writer, designer, or organizer. When you work directly with people, remember to continually cultivate your tranquility and flexibility; otherwise, you may come across as being haughty or angry. The important thing for you to remember if you are in a relationship is to learn how to assuage your anger and to truly honor your partner's opinions.

If Tiger is your yearly animal symbol, you are elegant, graceful, and talented. You have potential to do great things by helping others. Please cultivate your patience and do not be egotistical when you are in your flourishing time, otherwise, your life might take a turn for the worse.

If Tiger is your monthly animal symbol, you have very good fortune in your life. Your health situation is good and life is generally happy. You can easily accomplish your tasks. You can have a long, happy marriage.

If Tiger is your hourly animal symbol, you might have a thorny relationship with your family of origin, or be something of a troublemaker for your parents. It would be better to consider moving further away from your parents and your ancestral homeland. You have a hard life when you are young, but you can make a lot of money in your middle age. Make sure to take good care of yourself and practice some inner cultivation when you are 26, 29, 33, 39, 49, and 66 years old. During these years, you have potential susceptibilities for disorders related with *Qi* and blood. You can live till 95 years old if you work through these years.

**Tiger Landscape (Balance,
Communicate with Harmony)**

Pavilion rests your long march

Blossom rejoices over peaceful match

Tiger-Dragon communicate
with harmony

Universe celebrates for no worry

I will categorize some general Tiger features here for your further interest.

Personality

You are careful, graceful, powerful, enthusiastic, friendly, and attractive, and can sometimes be easily angered, have difficulties taking advice, or have challenges with authority. You take great vigilance before you move into actions that will help you to achieve your goals. You are vivacious, like fast growing spring bamboo shoots, which will help you to achieve your ambitions. Your emotions can also act just like bamboo in your garden, taking over all the space quickly if left uncontrolled. So, please practice being calm and flexible, in order to help you cool down your fiery desire. Managing your fiery nature will help you to reach your destination, no matter how difficult the situation may be.

Health

You have strong life energy and good health potential. It might weaken your immune system if you suffer from an unresolved grief. Also, being easy to anger can potentially cause a weakness of your gallbladder system and/or problems with your thyroid. Relax and cultivate more peace in your daily life; this will greatly benefit your health.

Relationships

A Horse, Dog, or Pig person may be your soul mate, or at least can be your very close friend. A Rabbit or Dragon person will make a great business partner for you. Be careful around a Snake person because it is easy to have some conflicts between the two of you. Try to make peace with a Monkey person – sometimes, you two get into fights for no real reason. You will have simple relationships with other animal symbol people.

Career

With your good leadership qualities and cautious character, you can suit yourself well as a writer, designer, or organizer, or as a self-employed person.

Finance

You have good luck with money. Not only can you easily make money by your efforts, but also you have some chance of getting money through an inheritance.

Color

Green is your spirit's original color, and will always help you feel deeply connected with your spirit. Red is the color that will help you find your own potential energy and talent. Dressing in red when you have an important social activity, such as public speaking or lecturing, will help bring your talents out. White will help you feel grounded. As yellow or brown are your financial colors, these two colors will bring you good luck in your finances – so have some of them in your office! Black is your spiritual source color, and having it in your cultivation room or bedroom will nourish your body physically and spiritually.

Food

White color vegetables, pungent spices (like garlic and onion), fermented foods, poultry, wild bird game, and mulberries are good for you.

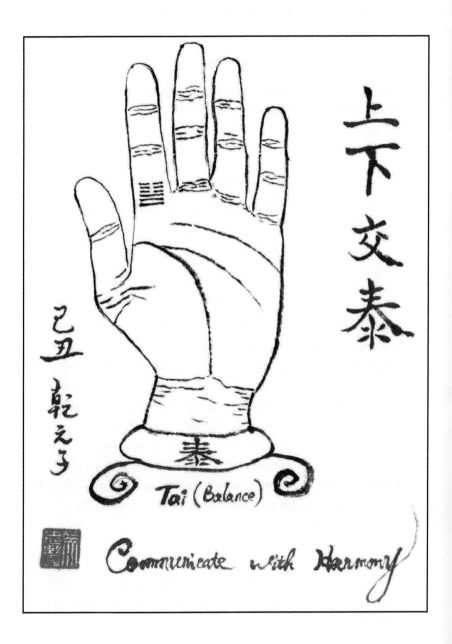

上下交泰

己丑 乾元子

泰

Tai (Balance)

Communicate with Harmony

Tai (Balance)

Tai is the tidal hexagram that represents the energetic pattern of the Tiger animal symbol. The Chinese character *Tai* means stable, great, maximal, safe, peaceful, luxurious, arrogant, and balance. The symbol of the hexagram is made with three *Yang* lines at the bottom and three *Yin* lines on top. This symbol represents *Yang Qi*, or life energy, getting stronger than the previous pattern *Lin*, in a natural cycle. The combination of three *Yin* lines and three *Yang* lines within the hexagram indicates the balance state of *Yin* and *Yang*. *Tai* represents the time or place where you can easily achieve your goal because you feel comfortable, peaceful, and harmonious.

In an annual cycle, *Tai* represents the *Yin* month, which occurs from approximately February 4 to March 6 in a solar calendar. This is the first month of the spring season according to Chinese cosmology. It is also the time that new sprouts and buds are growing, and when hibernating animals are awakening in certain parts of the northern hemisphere. It is the season where nature shows its new cycle starting. *Yin* symbolizes showing off your energy or talent during peaceful times or situations, just as it is the time when nature bursts forth with new life energy and shows off its beauty during the spring months. *Yin* also represents the wisdom of choosing the right environment to be able to accomplish your life mission.

In a daily cycle, *Tai* stands for *Yin* time, which is 03:00–04:59. This time period is comparable to the first month in spring, when hibernating animals are waking up. This is the time that you need to be active and awaken your consciousness. In general, it is the best cultivation time for all meditation and other inner cultivation practices.

Let us discover more information about *Tai* from *Yijing* wisdom. The hexagram *Tai* is made up of two trigrams: the top trigram is *Kun* (Earth) and the bottom trigram is *Qian* (Heaven). It is an image of Heaven below the Earth. Heaven is the symbol for circulating and strengthening new life energy or power. Again, Earth is the symbol for holding yourself stable or centering your mind. The hexagram *Tai* is a harmonious energetic pattern of Heaven and Earth, in which the Heavenly *Qi* (rain) is descending and the Earthly *Qi* is ascending. It is an image of a powerful person with a gentle attitude. *Tai* is also the image of you in meditation: steady your body and mind, then regulate your breathing to be slow, smooth, deep, and even. Bring your breath into your lower belly in order to circulate your *Qi*. This will allow you to feel your *Qi* free flowing in your body to maintain balance and peace in your whole physical and spiritual body.

The wisdom of the hexagram *Tai* (Balance) advises us that we should be gentle, soft, and humble with power and strength holding within, no matter who we are communicating with. It also tells us that a balanced or harmonious situation is always made with *Yin* energy embracing the *Yang* energy. This same principle applies to health as well. The reason that all the traditional Qigong forms have powerful healing functions is because the practices follow this *Tai* philosophy. I hope you can try some inner cultivation with me at *Tai* time; it is a time for you to be aware of your inner power and wisdom and to balance your life.

Inner Cultivation *Tai* ceremony

At any time when you need help bringing balance to your life, or when you want to enhance a current state of balance in your life, light a candle in front of you and start this meditation.

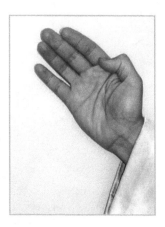

First straighten your back and feel that your body is stable like a mountain. Then, make the *Tai* mudra by placing each thumb on the palmar crease of the index finger. The palmar crease of the index finger is related to the hexagram *Tai*. Keeping your fingers relaxed and close together, please place your left palm on your lower belly, facing earth, close to your navel, and place your right palm, facing heaven, above your head. Adjust your breathing to be slow, smooth, deep, and even. Feel each breath connecting with your skin, small intestines, stomach, and gallbladder. Meditate as long as you can. Before ending, please say a little prayer:

"May the Spiritual Lights transform
all the grief energy to joy,

May the Spiritual Lights transform my
ego to have great compassion,

May the Spiritual Lights transform all conflicts
in the world to bring balance and peace."

4

Rabbit and *DaZhuang* 大壯 (Prosper)

T he rabbit has a quiet and gentle nature, and it looks cute. Rabbits give you a soft, easy going, slow, and stable feeling when they are quiet. But, once they start running, they are very fast and agile. They create an intricate system of dens which allows them to be good at staying hidden. Rabbits do not have sharp teeth, and they are not interested in fighting with others. In the Chinese tradition, the Rabbit is a symbol for wisdom, skill, ambition, humanity, and secrets. It is the fourth animal symbol in the 12 Chinese Animals System. We use *Mao* 卯 to represent the Rabbit symbol in the 12 Earthly Branches. *Mao* is a symbol for the 05:00–06:59 time of day, and for the second month in the Chinese Lunar-Solar calendar, which is approximately March 6 to April 5 in the Gregorian solar calendar. *Mao* represents the sunrise time of day and the spring blossom blooming month of the year. It is a time or a place where *Yang* energy (life energy) is getting into its strong stage in a new life cycle. We use the tidal hexagram *DaZhuang* to symbolize Rabbit.

Having a Rabbit animal symbol in your Chinese birth chart suggests you are clever, intelligent, skillful, agile, kind, and compassionate, and can sometimes be surreptitious or over-cautious. You have great awareness around knowing when it is time to take action and when it is time to have a rest, which will help you to work consistently to achieve your goals. You do not like to take risks in your life. You enjoy steady progress when getting your things done. Your cautious nature will allow you to continue your tasks to completion.

People love your tenderness and compassion. You will do well to choose a caring job, such as a nurse, gardener, concierge, designer, or healer. When you work directly with people, the only thing you need to do is show them your kind nature. It is not necessary to hold yourself back too much. The important thing for you to remember if you are in a relationship is to learn how to communicate with your partner directly.

If Rabbit is your yearly animal symbol, you will likely have an easy and steady life. Your business will stay firm. You reach your life peak in your middle age and stay comfortable there for a long time.

If Rabbit is your monthly animal symbol, you have great kindness. You could easily give forgiveness to others, even if someone did very bad things to you. You do not have any trouble with money throughout your whole life. You can be very rich when you are in your middle age. Sometimes, you may have lonely feelings because you live alone many years before you start your own family.

If Rabbit is your hourly animal symbol, you have a challenging life before your forties. You feel very comfortable after that challenging time period, and enjoy your retirement life. Make sure to take good care of yourself and meditate and pray on your eighteenth and twenty-sixth birthdays. During these two years, it is possible you may have a bad accident. Once those challenge years have passed, you might be able to live over 90 years.

Rabbit Landscape (Prosper, Uplift your Spirit)

Clear dew nourishes all beings

Fresh green reveals strong living

Powerful Thunder
roaring in Heaven

Joyful life singing
prosperous world

I will categorize some general Rabbit features here for your further interest.

Personality

You are clever, intelligent, skillful, agile, kind, and compassionate, and can sometimes be surreptitious or over-cautious. You are flourishing, like a big tree. Your compassion and wisdom will help you easily work through difficult times and achieve your greatest goals in life. The Chinese have a proverb – a great tree will first be knocked by the wind – meaning that people will give you trouble once you become famous. Therefore, please do not forget your careful natural tendency to cultivate your humbleness when you are successful or renowned.

Health

Generally speaking, you are in good shape and will live a long life. Please do not overwork and over drink! Otherwise, you might have liver and digestion problems.

Relationships

A Pig or Goat person may be your soul mate, or at least can be your very close friend. You have a good relationship with a Dog person. A Tiger person will make a great business partner for you. Be aware of a Dragon person: while it is easy to attract each other, there are some conflicts between you two. Try to make peace with a Rooster person – sometimes, you two may get into fights for no real reason. You will have simple relationships with other animal symbol people.

Career

With your tenderness and compassion, you are well suited to being a nurse, gardener, concierge, designer, healer, or spiritual leader.

Finance

You do not have trouble making money. You might become very rich when you reach middle age. You will likely have a comfortable retired life.

Color

Green is your spirit's original color, and will always help you feel deeply connected with your spirit. Red is the color that will help you find your own potential energy and talent. You should dress in red colors when you have an important social activity, such as public speaking or lecturing. A white color will help you feel grounded. As yellow or brown are your financial colors, it will bring you good luck in your finances to have these colors in your office. Black is your spiritual source color, and having it in your cultivation room or bedroom will nourish your body, physically and spiritually.

Food

Green vegetables, fermented foods, pork, lamb, and sour flavor foods are good for you.

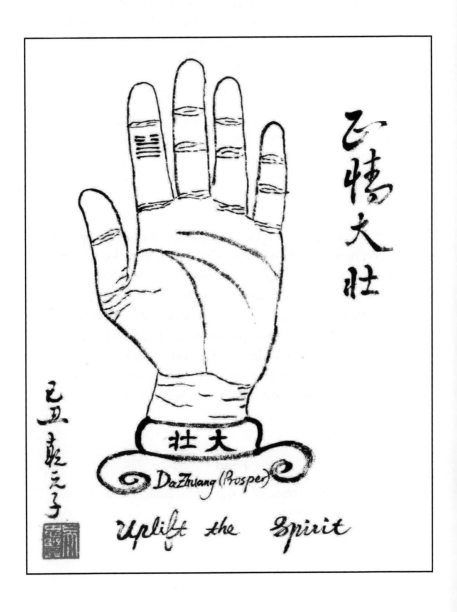

DaZhuang (Prosper)

Uplift the Spirit

DaZhuang (Prosper)

DaZhuang is the tidal hexagram that represents the energetic pattern of the Rabbit animal symbol. The two Chinese characters *DaZhuang* mean great strength, prevail, and prosper. The symbol of the hexagram is made with four *Yang* lines on the bottom and two *Yin* lines on top. This symbol represents *Yang Qi*, or life energy, getting stronger than the previous pattern *Tai*, in a natural cycle. The symbolic meaning of *DaZhuang* represents the time or place where you can expend your life energy or new business easily.

In an annual cycle, *DaZhuang* represents the *Mao* month, which occurs from approximately March 6 to April 5 in a solar calendar. This is the second month of the spring season according to Chinese cosmology. It is also the time that the weather is getting warm and nature is prospering in most areas in the northern hemisphere. This is when farmers work hard on their land. By now, most hibernating animals are completely awake. *Mao* symbolizes bursting forth your energy and talent in a right time or situation.

In a daily cycle, *DaZhuang* stands for *Mao* time, which is 05:00–06:59. This time period is comparable to the second month in spring, when nature is flourishing. This is the time that you should be very active and expand your power. It is one of the best cultivation times for you to strengthen your life energy and transform yourself into a prosperous state.

Let us discover more information about *DaZhuang* from *Yijing* wisdom. The hexagram *DaZhuang* is made up of two trigrams: the top trigram is *Zhen* (Thunder) and the bottom trigram is *Qian* (Heaven). It is an image of Thunder in the Heaven (sky).

Thunder is the symbol for creating new life energy or power. Again, Heaven is the symbol for strengthening yourself and being a great person. The hexagram *DaZhuang* is an image of spring thunder awakening the whole world. *DaZhuang* is also the image of you in meditation: your energy is getting very strong through your breathing technique, you can feel the *Qi* is nourishing your spirit and you can hear the thunder roaring in your head.

The wisdom of the hexagram *DaZhuang* (Prosper) advises that it is best to get things done when we are in good circumstances. It also counsels us to take advantage and take charge when opportunities present themselves. Your daily cultivation will help you maintain well-being and prosperity. I hope you can try some inner cultivation with me at *DaZhuang* time; it is a time for you to be great and illuminated.

Inner Cultivation *DaZhuang* ceremony

At any time when you need help to find your strength, or you would like to maintain your flourishing life, light a candle in front of you and start this meditation.

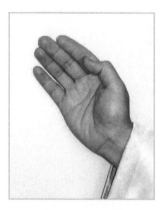

First straighten your back and feel that your body is stable like a mountain. Then, make the *DaZhuang* mudra by placing each thumb on the second crease of the index finger. The second crease of the index finger is related to the hexagram *DaZhuang*. Keeping your fingers relaxed and close together, place your fingers by your ears with palms facing forwards, and seal your ear with your middle finger. Adjust your breathing to be slow, smooth, deep, and even. Feel each breath connecting with your large intestines and liver. Meditate as long as you can. Before ending, please say a little prayer:

"May the Spiritual Lights transform my
physical body into the Qi body,

May the Spiritual Lights transform my
Qi body into the spiritual body,

May the Spiritual Lights transform my
spiritual body into the Great Dao."

5

Dragon and
Guai 夬
(Transform)

龍辰
決剛夬
有利柔
往攸

戊子軒之

Dragon is the only legendary and mystical animal in the 12 Chinese Animals System – as far as I know, no one has ever seen a real living dragon. The physical image and symbolic meaning of the Chinese dragon is different from the understanding of the dragon in the West. In Chinese shamanism, Dragon is an auspicious animal. It stands for transformation, communication, connection, freedom, and the universal way. Dragon is also the rainmaker, has magic powers to change natural formations, and can easily fly between Heaven and Earth. Dragon can penetrate through rock or other matter without hindrance. Dragon lives in the rock, just as fish lives in the water and human being lives in the air.

Dragon is the fifth animal symbol in the 12 Chinese Animals System. We use *Chen* 辰 to represent the Dragon symbol in the 12 Earthly Branches. *Chen* is a symbol for the 07:00–08:59 time of day, and for the third month in the Chinese Lunar-Solar calendar, which is approximately April 5 to May 6 in the Gregorian solar calendar. *Chen* represents the breakfast time of day and the third spring month, when nature is in its most magical transformative season. It is a time or a place where *Yang* energy (life energy) is growing fast and making dramatic changes in a new life cycle. We use the tidal hexagram *Guai* to symbolize Dragon.

Having a Dragon animal symbol in your Chinese birth chart suggests you are powerful, mystical, straight, healthy, congenial, and elegant, and can sometimes be emotional, critical, or unhappy.

You have an active imagination and artistic nature, which will help you achieve your goals. You have a tendency to change your mind easily and may give up easily when you encounter some difficulties in your work. It will help you to complete your tasks if you learn to listen to others and think things over very carefully before you take a new step in your life.

You would do well to choose an imaginative job, such as designing, constructing, painting, music, or advertising. When you work directly with people, you would be wise to continually cultivate your stability; otherwise, you may waste your time or come across as being untrustworthy. The most important thing for you to remember if you are going to have a relationship is to deliberate your decisions, and be very clear that you will truly commit yourself to them.

If Dragon is your yearly animal symbol, you will likely have an unstable life, particularly when you are young. You move around here and there and try different possibilities for your future. However, you are able to achieve your goals and be successful in business if you can plan and be intentional with your thoughts and commit to that which you really like to do.

If Dragon is your monthly animal symbol, you have a big heart and great sympathy for others. You have a triumphant life when you are in your thirties. In later decades, you will have a lovely and noble life.

If Dragon is your hourly animal symbol, you are smart and talented. You can make a good amount of money when you are young. You have more challenges in life during your middle age, and you have a glowing life after working through those challenges. Make sure to take good care of yourself and have nice vacations when you are 19, 27, 36, and 39 years old. You might have an accident in these potentially difficult years. Be careful when you are 75 years old because you might have a major health problem at this time.

**Dragon Landscape (Transform,
Change to the Great Path)**

Magical Dragons dancing
in black clouds

Legendary Pearl hides red sun

Auspicious transformation
playing the sky

Great Path awaits through mist

I will categorize some general Dragon features here for your further interest.

Personality

You are powerful, mystical, straight, healthy, congenial, and elegant, and can sometimes be emotional, critical, or unhappy. You are changeable, like clouds in the sky. Your romantic and artistic character needs to be balanced by centering yourself well, which will help you complete your tasks and achieve your greatest goals in life.

Health

In general, you have a pretty healthy life. Please give yourself at least a half-hour exercise time every day. Otherwise, you may become uncomfortably heavy when you get to your early forties. Eat well and sleep well to avoid having concerns about your digestion and kidney health.

Relationships

A Monkey, Rooster, or Rat person may be your soul mate, or at least can be your very close friend. A Tiger person will make a great business partner for you. Be careful around a Rabbit person because it is easy to have some conflicts between you two, even though the two of you may sometimes feel as close as siblings. Try to make peace with a Dog person – sometimes, you two get into fights for no real reason. You will have simple relationships with other animal symbol people.

Career

With your imaginative and artistic nature, you can suit yourself as a designer, constructor, painter, musician, or engineer, or in advertising.

Finance

You have good opportunities to make money. You might become very rich if you can be consistent and do what you really like. In general, winter is a good season for you to increase your financial power.

Color

Yellow or brown are your spirit's original colors, and will always help you feel deeply connected with your spirit. White is the color that will help you find your own potential energy and talent. You should wear white clothes when you have an important social activity, such as public speaking or lecturing. Green will help you feel grounded. As black is your financial color, it will bring you good luck in your finances to have some black in your office. Red is your spiritual source color, and having it in your cultivation room or bedroom will nourish your body physically and spiritually.

Food

Green vegetables, soybeans, black beans, fermented foods, sea vegetables, and fish are good for you.

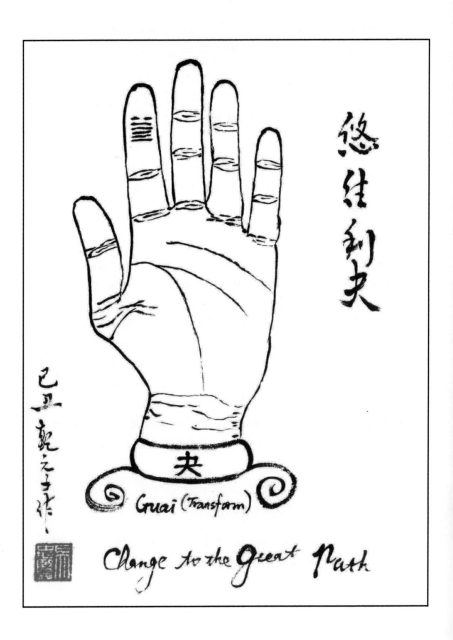

Guai (Transform)

Change to the Great Path

Guai (Transform)

Guai is the tidal hexagram that represents the energetic pattern of the Dragon animal symbol. The Chinese character Guai means decide, dredge, dig, burst, and transform. The symbol of the hexagram is made with five Yang lines on the bottom with one Yin line on top. This symbol represents Yang Qi, or life energy, getting stronger than the previous pattern DaZhuang in a natural cycle. The symbolic meaning of Guai is similar to an overflowing reservoir that needs to be drained immediately, lest the dam breaks. It represents the time or place where you are in power and you should control yourself well; be sure to deliberate and do not make major decisions arbitrarily.

In an annual cycle, Guai represents the Chen month, which occurs from approximately April 5 to May 6 in a solar calendar. This is the last month of the spring season according to Chinese cosmology. It is also the time when nature is getting ready for the summer season in the northern hemisphere. The first day of this month is Qingming 清明, a special festival to connect with nature and ancestral energy in old Chinese traditions. When I was young, like almost everyone in my hometown area, I dressed up and carried colorful papers, incense, and fireworks with my family to visit my ancestors' graveyard during Qingming. After we cleared the weeds, we decorated our ancestral tombs with colorful paper, and then burnt the incense and made the fireworks to pray to the Heaven, Earth, and ancestral spirits, asking for peace, health, and good luck for the family. Although I have not had a chance to return to my hometown to celebrate this special festival physically, my spirit wanders back there and dances in the colorful mountain with the fireworks as I recall that time. Qingming literally means pure brightness. The festival represents the season when we need to purify our old energy and remember where we came from by visiting nature and our ancestors' tombs, in order to help us to see our future clearly.

Chen symbolizes making a good decision for your future during the most influential time or situation. *Chen* also represents the wisdom of first purifying your body, mind, and spirit before making a new transformation.

In a daily cycle, *Guai* stands for *Chen* time, which is 07:00– 08:59. This time period is comparable to the last month in spring, when nature has its great transformation – young plants are entering their mature stage, fruit trees are yielding and their blossom petals are falling down. This is the time that you should give yourself new nourishment to get ready for the next stage of your life.

Let us discover more information about *Guai* from *Yijing* wisdom. The hexagram *Guai* is made up of two trigrams: the top trigram is *Dui* (Lake) and the bottom trigram is *Qian* (Heaven). It is an image of a Lake over the Heaven. Lake is the symbol for changing old patterns and transformation into new life energy or power. Heaven is the symbol for the circulation of planets, motivating or strengthening yourself and being a great person. Combined, the hexagram *Guai* becomes an image of a great transformation based on the power of Heaven – unbroken, circulating, and spiraling. *Guai* is also the image of you in meditation. When the powerful *Qi* is circulating within your body constantly, you can feel a great transformation happening in your body; in the mean time, you can also feel your mouth full of aromatic saliva, just like a great nectar lake nourishing your physical and spiritual body.

The wisdom of the hexagram *Guai* (Transform) advises us that we should purify and change the old patterns when we are experiencing times of great strength. This is the time to transform, when the situation is most favorable. If we take advantage of the circumstances, we will not miss the golden opportunity. An unwavering attitude will help us accomplish our tasks, even if we bump into some tough situations. I hope you can try some inner cultivation with me at *Guai* time; it is a time for you to transform your inner power and awaken your deepest consciousness.

Inner Cultivation *Guai* ceremony

At any time when you need help to make a new transition, or you are in a power situation, light a candle in front of you and start this meditation.

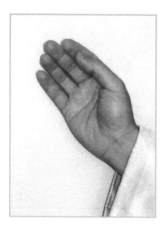

First straighten your back and feel that your body is stable like a mountain. Then, make the *Guai* mudra by placing each thumb on the top crease of the index finger. The top crease of the index finger is related to the hexagram *Guai*. Keeping your fingers relaxed and close together, place your mudras on your knees with palms facing up. Adjust your breathing to be slow, smooth, deep, and even. Feel each breath connecting with your stomach, kidney, and liver. Meditate as long as you can. Before ending, please say a little prayer:

"May the Spiritual Lights transform my
organs' Qi to nourish my spirit,

May the Spiritual Lights transform
my Three Flowers into One,*

May the Spiritual Lights transform my saliva
into nectar nourishing my body and heart."

---

* In Chinese inner cultivation, Three Flowers means the *Jing* (essence), *Qi* (vital energy), and *Shen* (spirit); One means Dao, the Great Way.

6

Snake and *Qian* 乾 (Strengthen)

乾元亨利貞萬
國咸寧

巳蛇
戊子冬

The snake has cold and slippery skin. Snakes always move calmly and cautiously, and act very sharply and quickly once they snap up their prey. In the Chinese tradition, Snake is a symbol for wisdom, caution, intuition, attraction, intelligence, and mysticism. It is the sixth animal symbol in the 12 Chinese Animals System. We use *Si* 巳 to represent the Snake symbol in the 12 Earthly Branches. *Si* is a symbol for the 09:00–10:59 time of day, and for the fourth month in the Chinese Lunar-Solar calendar, which is approximately May 6 to June 6 in the Gregorian solar calendar. *Si* represents morning in the daily cycle, and the first month of summer in the yearly cycle. It can represent either a time or a place in which *Yang* energy (life energy) is reaching its peak stage in a new life cycle. We use the tidal hexagram *Qian* to symbolize Snake.

Having a Snake animal symbol in your Chinese birth chart suggests that you are cautious, intuitive, wise, sympathetic, and attractive. It is also common for Snake people to be conceited, insatiable, or sluggish. As a Snake animal person, you have great prudence and wisdom, which will help you to achieve your goals. You have patience to get things done once you have a long-term plan formulated. You would be wise to cultivate the ability to be open: it will allow your internal warmth and enthusiasm to be felt when you communicate with others.

Sharing your inner warmth will help you feel more supported when you communicate with people.

Generally speaking, you have a pretty smooth life. People like your softness and graceful manner. You would do well to choose an artistic job, like being an artist, writer, designer, or teacher. When you work directly with people, remember to continually cultivate your warmness and humbleness; otherwise, you may come across as being egotistical or greedy. The important thing for you to remember if you are in a relationship is to learn how to express your feelings to your partner.

If Snake is your yearly animal symbol, you are elegant, knowledgeable, and wise. You have potential to do great things by educating or advising others. Please cultivate your warmth and do not close yourself off when you have a conflict with others.

If Snake is your monthly animal symbol, you have pretty good fortune in your life. Your health situation is good. You can tell your life is getting better and better as time passes. You can accomplish your tasks if you do not give up. You have some challenges in your life when you are young, and have a flowering life after those challenges. You have a long, harmonious marriage.

If Snake is your hourly animal symbol, you are smart and graceful. You are rich even when you are pretty young. You might feel grief around your relationship with your family. Make sure to take good care of yourself and practice some inner cultivation when you are 31, 36, 49, and 74 years old. During these years, you have potential susceptibilities for sickness or accidents.

**Snake Landscape (Strengthen,
Run with the Heavenly Way)**

Forked tongue ready for prey

Glowing eye sees the Way

Flexible body yields
unlimited power

Gentle spirit kindles
ocean wisdom

I will categorize some general Snake features here for your further interest.

Personality

You are cautious, intuitive, wise, sympathetic, and attractive. It is also common for Snake people to be conceited, insatiable, or sluggish. You are particularly watchful before you proceed with actions, which helps you to achieve your goals. Your calm and enthusiastic nature will help you achieve your dreams. Sometimes, you hold your emotions inside, which may give people the wrong impression that you are a cold person, just like the snake has cold skin. So, please practice being open, in order to help you easily communicate with people.

Health

You have an easy life and good health potential. It might weaken your circulation system if you overthink about an unresolved project, or if you overeat and drink.

Relationships

A Monkey, Rooster, or Ox person may be your soul mate, or at least can be your very close friend. A Horse or Goat person will make a great business partner for you. Be careful around a Tiger person because it is easy to have some conflicts between the two of you. Try to make peace with a Pig person – sometimes, you may get into fights for no real reason. You will have simple relationships with other animal symbol people.

Career

With your softness and wise character, you will be well suited as an artist, writer, designer, or teacher.

Finance

You have a good ability to make money. You should have a rich life if you do not take too many risks investing your money.

Color

Red is your spirit's original color, and will always help you feel deeply connected with your spirit. Yellow or brown are the colors that will help you find your own potential energy and talent. Dressing in yellow and/or brown colors when you have an important social activity, such as public speaking or lecturing, will help accentuate your talents. Black will help you feel grounded. As white is your financial color, it will bring you good luck in your finances – so have some white in your office! Green is your spiritual source color, and having it in your cultivation room or bedroom will nourish your body physically and spiritually.

Food

Grain, sweet spices (like licorice), root vegetables, honey, chicken, and fruit are good for you. But please never overeat.

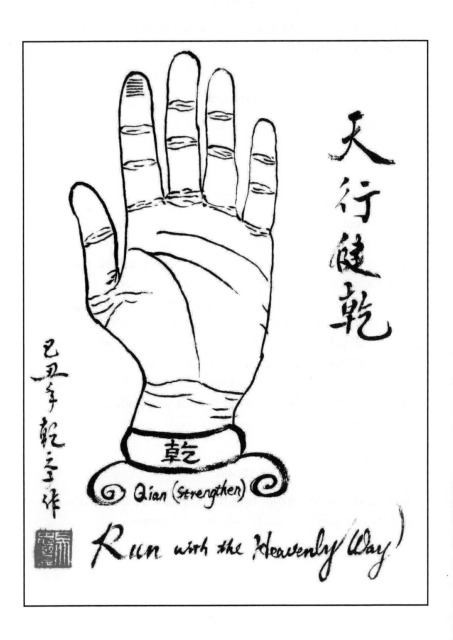

乾

Qian (Strengthen)

Run with the Heavenly Way

Qian (Strengthen)

Qian is the tidal hexagram that represents the energetic pattern of the Snake animal symbol. The Chinese character Qian means strong, dry, uprising, unbroken, perfect, and strengthen. The symbol of the hexagram is made with three Yang lines at the bottom and three Yang lines on top. This symbol represents Yang Qi, or life energy, getting stronger than the previous pattern Guai, in a natural cycle. The combination of six Yang lines within the hexagram indicates a completing or peak state of Yang. Qian represents the time or place where you are in the top position.

In an annual cycle, Qian represents the Si month, which occurs from approximately May 6 to June 6 in a solar calendar. This is the first month of the summer season according to Chinese cosmology. It is also the time that plants are flowering and maturing, and hibernating animals are completely awake in the northern hemisphere. It is the season where nature shows its prosperity. Si symbolizes showing off your energy or talent, just as it is the time when nature shows off its luxury during the summer time. Si also represents the wisdom of expressing your power and strength at the opportune moment.

In a daily cycle, Qian stands for Si time, which is 09:00–10:59. This time period is comparable to the first month in summer, when nature is thriving. This is the time that you should be active and totally awaken your consciousness. In general, it is the best time for getting things done.

Let us discover more information about Qian from Yijing wisdom. The hexagram Qian is made up of two trigrams: the top trigram is Qian (Heaven) and the bottom trigram is Qian (Heaven). It is an image of Heaven over Heaven. Heaven is the symbol for circulating and strengthening new life energy or power. The hexagram *Qian* is a dominant energetic pattern of nature, in which the Heavenly *Qi* continually runs without stopping to rest. It is the image of a person fulfilling a powerful duty. *Qian* is also the image of you in meditation: you never stop your daily practice. With this constant practice, your *Qi* is free flowing, and able to maintain balance and peace in your whole physical and spiritual body.

The wisdom of the hexagram *Qian* (Strengthen) advises us that we should be strong in physical, mental, and spiritual levels no matter what the circumstances are. The six unbroken lines in the hexagram indicate that we should continue our study and work and never be lazy. This same principle applies to health as well. We should never stop our daily inner cultivation. I hope you can try some inner cultivation with me at *Qian* time; it is a time for you to be completely aware of your inner power and wisdom.

Inner Cultivation *Qian* ceremony

At any time when you need help to strengthen your life, or when you are in your prosperous time of life, light a candle in front of you and start this meditation.

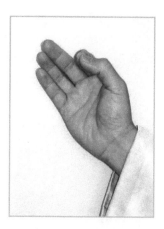

First straighten your back and feel that your body is stable like a mountain. Then, make the *Qian* mudra by placing each thumb on the tip of the index finger. The tip of the index finger is related to the hexagram *Qian*. Keeping your fingers relaxed and close together, please bring your hands above your head with palms facing each other, with your fingers gently touching. Adjust your breathing to be slow, smooth, deep, and even. Feel each breath connecting with your spleen, intestines, and the entire body. Meditate as long as you can. Before ending, please say a little prayer:

*"May the Spiritual Lights transform my
five organs' Qi to Five Color Lights,*[*]

*May the Spiritual Lights transform my Five
Color Lights into their Original Source,*[**]

*May the Spiritual Lights transform the Original
Source to deepen my humble nature."*

---

[*]   Five Color Lights refers to green, red, yellow, white, and black colors, which
        correspond to liver, heart, spleen, lung, and kidney, respectively.

[**]   Original Source means prenatal consciousness, which originates in Dao.

7

Horse and *Gou* 媾 (Copulate)

The horse has great endurance and power, yet it is very gentle. Horses give you a serene and friendly feeling when they are quiet. Once they are running, however, they are incredibly fast and powerful. In the Chinese tradition, Horse is a symbol for leadership, power, fashion, success, and passion. It is the seventh animal symbol in the 12 Chinese Animals System. We use *Wu* 午 to represent the Horse symbol in the 12 Earthly Branches. *Wu* is a symbol for the 11:00–12:59 time of day, and for the fifth month in the Chinese Lunar-Solar calendar, which is approximately June 6 to July 7 in the Gregorian solar calendar. *Wu* represents noon during the day and the summer fruiting season of the year. It is a time or a place where *Yang* energy (life energy) is just starting to decline after its strongest stage in a life cycle. We use the tidal hexagram *Gou* to symbolize Horse.

Having a Horse animal symbol in your Chinese birth chart suggests you are enduring, powerful, friendly, lively, and passionate, and can sometimes be agitated, irritable, or arrogant. You have great openness and enthusiasm, which will help you to achieve your goals. It is easy for you to get excited about new projects. Your enduring nature will allow you to continue your tasks to completion.

People love your openness and camaraderie. You would do well to choose physically arduous work, such as a landscaper, construction worker, surgeon, long distance truck driver, pilot, or certain government official. When you work directly with people, the only thing you need to remember is to continue sharing your friendly nature with them. The important thing for you to keep in mind if you are in a relationship is to learn to communicate with your partner, heart to heart.

If Horse is your yearly animal symbol, you will likely have an exciting life. Your business will be successful when you are young. You will be great if you endure, and never give up when difficulties arise in your life.

If Horse is your monthly animal symbol, you have great humanity and a successful life. You can easily get support from others when you need it. Throughout your entire life, you do not have any trouble with money. You may come into huge amounts of unexpected money.

If Horse is your hourly animal symbol, you have a harmonious life. You have a rich life, with much less struggle than your parents had. Make sure to take good care of yourself when you are 13, 32, 36, 49, and 78. During these years, it is possible that you may feel sick or be involved in a bad accident. A vegetarian diet, meditation, praying, and helping others without asking for rewards will help you to pass through these years.

Horse Landscape (Copulate, Unify Feminine and Masculine)

Butterflies flutter in romantic air

Purple flowering an
awakened spirit

Harmonious Wind flows
under Heaven

Steady mind unifying
Water and Fire

I will categorize some general Horse features here for your further interest.

Personality

You are enduring, powerful, friendly, lively, and passionate, and can sometimes be agitated, irritable, or arrogant. Your great openness and enthusiasm will help you easily work through difficult times and achieve your greatest goals in life. Please do not forget your natural enduring quality: it will help you to move forward when you are in difficult situations.

Health

Generally speaking, you are in good health and have a happy life. Please do not overstimulate yourself by the exciting things in your life. Otherwise, you might have problems with your heart and kidney systems.

Relationships

A Goat, Tiger or Dog person may be your soul mate, or at least can be your very close friend. A Snake person will make a great business partner for you. Be aware of an Ox person – while it is easy to attract each other, there are some conflicts between you two. Try to make peace with a Rat person – sometimes, you may get into fights for no real reason. You will have simple relationships with other animal symbol people.

Career

With your endurance and passion, you can suit yourself as a landscaper, construction worker, surgeon, long distance truck driver, pilot, or government officer.

Finance

You do not have trouble making money. You might become very rich, even when you are young.

Color

Red is your spirit's original color, and will always help you feel deeply connected with your spirit. Yellow or brown are the colors that will help you find your own potential energy and talent. You should dress in yellow and/or brown colors when you have an important social activity, such as public speaking or lecturing. Black will help you feel grounded. As white is your financial color, it will bring you good luck in your finances to have some white in your office. Green is your spiritual source color, and having it in your cultivation room or bedroom will nourish your body, physically and spiritually.

Food

Green vegetables, bitter flavor foods, lamb, and fish are good for you.

Gou (copulate)

Unify Feminine & Masculine

Gou (Copulate)

Gou is the tidal hexagram that represents the energetic pattern of the Horse animal symbol. The Chinese character *Gou* means join, mate, and copulate. The symbol of the hexagram is made with five *Yang* lines on top and one *Yin* line on the bottom. This symbol represents *Yang Qi*, or life energy, declining after the previous pattern *Qian*, in a natural cycle. The symbolic meaning of *Gou* represents the time or place where you should think about spending more time with your family and reduce your business activities.

In an annual cycle, *Gou* represents the *Wu* 午 month, which occurs from approximately June 6 to July 7 in a solar calendar. This is the second month of the summer season according to Chinese cosmology. It is also the time that the weather is hot and fruits are full in most areas in the northern hemisphere. *Wu* means *Yin* and *Yang* energies arc dancing together between the Heaven and Earth, which symbolizes holding your energy within after you reach the peak of your life.

DuanWu 端午 Festival (known as the Dragon Boat Festival in the West) and the summer solstice appear in this period. *DuanWu* 端午 is a traditional Chinese festival, originating from a Totem celebration of a tribe from Southeast China. It has since been celebrated for thousands of years in various ways. The *DuanWu* Festival represents Universal *Yang* energy "up-rising" or ascending. In the area of my hometown (in Southeast China), people drink wine made from *Xionghuang* 雄黃 (a Chinese herb with strong *Yang Qi*). At the *Wu* 午 (noon) of *DuanWu*, we make a paste with the *xionghuang* powder and place it in children's navels to strengthen their *Yang Qi*. After a few days of the *Yang Qi* "up-rising" in *DuanWu*, during the summer solstice, your internal *Yang Qi* will completely leave the deepest level of your energetic body and express itself in the outer layer of your body. Therefore, you must learn how to hold your *Yang Qi* within at the summer solstice. It will be good for your *Yang Qi* and digestive function if you can have a cup of warming ginger tea and do some inner Fire meditation during the summer solstice.

In a daily cycle, *Gou* stands for *Wu* time, which is 11:00–12:59. This time period is comparable to the second month in summer, when nature is full of fruits. This is the time to reduce your activities and withdraw your power. It is one of the best cultivation times for you to seize your life energy and transform yourself into a peaceful state.

Let us discover more information about *Gou* from *Yijing* wisdom. The hexagram *Gou* is made up of two trigrams: the top trigram is *Qian* (Heaven) and the bottom trigram is *Xun* (Wind). It is an image of Wind blowing under the Heaven (sky). Again, Heaven is the symbol for strengthening yourself and being a great person. Wind is the symbol for breath, life energy, and harmony. The hexagram *Gou* is an image of wind blustering the whole world. *Gou* is also the image of you in meditation. Your energy is very strong through your breathing technique; you can feel the *Qi* is nourishing your spirit and spreading throughout your whole body.

The wisdom of the hexagram *Gou* (Copulate) advises that it is best to let it be, to hold your strength within, allowing yourself some rest after you have achieved your goal. It also counsels us to enjoy family time. I hope you can try some inner cultivation with me at *Gou* time; it is a time for you to be soft and relax.

Inner Cultivation *Gou* ceremony

At any time when you need help to calm yourself, or you would like to reconsider your future direction, light a candle in front of you and start this meditation.

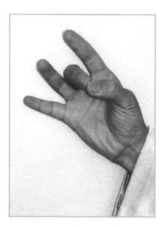

First straighten your back and feel that your body is stable like a mountain. Then, make the *Gou* mudra by placing each thumb on the tip of the middle finger. The tip of the middle finger is related to the hexagram *Gou*. Opening and relaxing your fingers, place your left hand in front of your chest and your right hand in front of your lower belly. Adjust your breathing to be slow, smooth, deep, and even. Feel each breath connecting with your small intestines and heart. Meditate as long as you can. Before ending, please say a little prayer:

"May the Spiritual Lights shine on my tranquil heart,
May the Spiritual Lights shine on my illumined spirit,
May the Spiritual Lights shine on
the harmonious world."

8

Goat and *Dun* 遁 (Retreat)

三 未羊
遯 亨也
與 時行
浸 而長

戊子輊夂

Goats give you gentle and peaceful feelings when they chew grass with a slow, grinding motion. Yet they move with great speed and agility when navigating their way through rough, rocky, mountainous areas. They have strong horns and are always ready to defeat their enemies. Goat is the eighth animal symbol in the 12 Chinese Animals System. We use *Wei* 未 to represent the Goat symbol in the 12 Earthly Branches. *Wei* is a symbol for the 13:00–14:59 time of day, and for the sixth month in the Chinese Lunar-Solar calendar, which is approximately July 7 to August 8 in the Gregorian solar calendar. *Wei* represents the napping time of day and the third summer month when nature is in its ripest season. It is a time or a place where *Yang* energy (life energy) is in further decline and when the life cycle becomes more mellow. We use the tidal hexagram *Dun* to symbolize Goat.

Having a Goat animal symbol in your Chinese birth chart suggests you are endurable, tender, courteous, gracious, and charming, and can sometimes be sorrowful, imaginary, or stubborn. You have an affectionate, vital, and peaceful nature, which will help you to achieve your goals. You have a tendency to over-trust your own opinion, and sometimes you might not want to listen to other people. It will be helpful when completing your tasks if you can listen to others and think things over before you take a new step in your life.

You would do well to choose a job that requires constant effort, such as an engineer, accountant, realtor, educator, writer, or doctor, or being self-employed. When you work directly with people, you would be wise to continually cultivate your flexibility; otherwise, you may come across as being stubborn. The most important thing for you to remember if you are going to have a relationship is to let it be.

If Goat is your yearly animal symbol, you will likely have a wobbly life. You have a tendency to move around here and there, pursuing different opportunities for your future. However, you are able to achieve your goals and be successful in business once you commit yourself to something you really like to do.

If Goat is your monthly animal symbol, you have a great artistic potential and are very elegant. You have a glorious life in general.

If Goat is your hourly animal symbol, you have a more challenging life. You might suffer the sorrow of losing connection with your family, or have a difficult partner relationship. You can make a good amount of money when you are young. You have destabilizing and shocking experiences during your middle age, and you will have a pretty good retirement. Make sure to take good care of yourself and have nice vacations when you are 19, 29, and 56 years old. Be very careful when you are 73 years old because you might have a major health problem at this time.

**Goat Landscape (Retreat, Hold
Back until the Time is Right)**

Sacred peak of Sacred Mountains
Hidden Immortal is
hiding within
Oh, any mountain under Heaven
Serene home of your return

I will categorize some general Goat features here for your further interest.

Personality

You are enduring, tender, courteous, gracious, and charming, and can sometimes be sorrowful, imaginary, or stubborn. You are steady, like mountains on the earth. Your endurance and gentle character will help you to complete your tasks and achieve your greatest goals in life.

Health

In general, you have a pretty healthy life. Please give yourself at least a half-hour exercise time every day. Otherwise, you may become uncomfortably heavy when you get to your late forties. Eat well and sleep well to avoid having concerns about your digestion, heart, and kidney health.

Relationships

A Pig, Rabbit, or Horse person may be your soul mate, or at least can be your very close friend. A Snake person will make a great business partner for you. Be careful around a Rat person because it is easy to have some conflicts between you two, even though the two of you may sometimes feel as close as siblings. Try to make peace with an Ox person – sometimes, you may get into fights for no real reason. You will have simple relationships with other animal symbol people.

Career

With your fortitude and moderate nature, you can suit yourself as an engineer, accountant, realtor, educator, writer, or doctor, or be self-employed.

Finance

You have good opportunities to make money. You can have a very comfortable life without worrying about finances. In general, winter is a good season for you to increase your financial power.

Color

Yellow or brown are your spirit's original colors, and will always help you feel deeply connected with your spirit. White is the color that will help you find your own potential energy and talent. You should wear white clothes when you have an important social activity, such as public speaking or lecturing. Green will help you feel grounded. As black is your financial color, it will bring you good luck in your finances to have some black in your office. Red is your spiritual source color, and having it in your cultivation room or bedroom will nourish your body physically and spiritually.

Food

Green vegetables, soybeans, black beans, fermented foods, lamb, and fish are good for you.

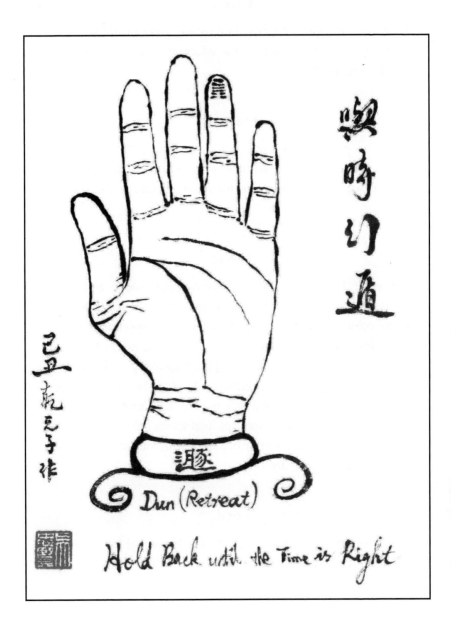

Dun (Retreat)

Hold Back until the Time is Right

Dun (Retreat)

Dun is the tidal hexagram that represents the energetic pattern of the Goat animal symbol. The Chinese character *Dun* means withdraw, hide, conceal, and retreat. The symbol of the hexagram is made with four *Yang* lines on the bottom and two *Yin* lines on top. This symbol represents *Yang Qi*, or life energy, declining further than the previous pattern *Gou*, in a natural cycle. It represents the time or place where you should take off and be ready for your next life stage. *Dun* represents the wisdom of recharging your body, mind, and spirit even when you are still in your prosperous life stage.

In an annual cycle, *Dun* represents the *Wei* month, which occurs from approximately July 7 to August 8 in a solar calendar. This is the last month of the summer season according to Chinese cosmology. It is also the time when nature is getting ready for the autumn season in the northern hemisphere.

In a daily cycle, *Dun* stands for *Wei* time, which is 13:00–14:59. This time period is comparable to the last month in summer, when nature has reached its greatest maturation – plants are full of leaves and ripened fruit. This is the time to give yourself a break in order to get ready for the next stage of your life.

Let us discover more information about *Dun* from *Yijing* wisdom. The hexagram *Dun* is made up of two trigrams: the top trigram is *Qian* (Heaven) and the bottom trigram is *Gen* (Mountain). It is an image of a mountain under the Heaven. Heaven is the symbol for the circulation of planets, motivating or strengthening yourself, and being a great person. A mountain represents the stability and spiritual quality of the trigram *Gen*. It indicates that in our daily life, we need to have internal stability, just like a mountain. Combined, the hexagram *Dun* becomes an image of a great hermit life – staying in the mountain to cultivate the Way of Heaven, the compassion, gentleness, and peace. *Dun* is also the image of you in meditation: when the powerful *Qi* is circulating within your body constantly, you still need to stabilize your body, breath, and mind like a mountain.

The wisdom of the hexagram *Dun* (Retreat) advises us that we should withdraw ourselves from a high position or cultivate more humbleness after we have achieved our greatest goals. This is the time to rejuvenate, and never to overdo things. If we steadily prepare for a peaceful future during the times we are in a great situation, we will never feel miserable. I hope you can try some inner cultivation with me at *Dun* time; it is a time for you to look and listen within, to gain insight into how to create your greatest future.

Inner Cultivation *Dun* ceremony

At any time when you need help to rejuvenate, or you are on top of your game and in a situation of power, light a candle in front of you and start this meditation.

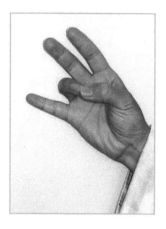

First straighten your back and feel that your body is stable like a mountain. Then, make the *Dun* mudra by placing each thumb on the tip of the ring finger. The tip of the ring finger is related to the hexagram *Dun*. Opening and relaxing your fingers, place your right mudra on your right knee with palm facing up and raise your left mudra close to your left shoulder with palm facing forward. Adjust your breathing to be slow, smooth, deep, and even. Feel each breath connecting with your spleen, heart, and liver. Meditate as long as you can. Before ending, please say a little prayer:

"May the Spiritual Lights shine on my unwavering mind,
May the Spiritual Lights shine on my unbroken breath,
May the Spiritual Lights shine on my unpolluted body."

9

Monkey and
Pi 否 (Break)

猴

戊子新春

否君子
以儉德
辟難不
可榮祿

The monkey has an agile body and a nimble mind. Monkeys always carefully observe the situation, making sure they will not be trapped or captured by hunters before they take their food. In the Chinese tradition, Monkey is a symbol for wit, watchfulness, spontaneity, elegance, opportunism, and supervision. It is the ninth animal symbol in the 12 Chinese Animals System. We use *Shen* 申 to represent the Monkey symbol in the 12 Earthly Branches. *Shen* is a symbol for the 15:00–16:59 time of day, and for the seventh month in the Chinese Lunar-Solar calendar, which is approximately August 8 to September 8 in the Gregorian solar calendar. In the daily cycle, *Shen* represents the afternoon, the time to finish your day's work, and the first month of autumn in the yearly cycle. It can represent either a time or a place in which *Yang* energy (life energy) is further declining and breaking down to half of its peak stage in a life cycle. We use the tidal hexagram *Pi* to symbolize Monkey.

Having a Monkey animal symbol in your Chinese birth chart suggests that you are intelligent, attentive, spontaneous, smart, elegant, and wise. It is also common for Monkey people to be opportunistic, silly, or rushed. As a Monkey animal person, you have nimble wits and wisdom, which will help you to achieve your goals. You can easily get what you want once you have a plan formulated. You would be wise to cultivate your patience because it might take a little longer than you expected to achieve your goals. Generally speaking, you have a very good life. People like your intelligence and leadership. You would do well to choose a prominent job, like being a director, contractor, teacher, designer, or a leader in the community. When you work directly with people, remember to continually cultivate your patience and humbleness; otherwise, you may come across as being haughty or irascible. The important thing for you to remember if you are in a relationship is to learn how to communicate with your partner, and do not take it personally when your partner has frustrations.

If Monkey is your yearly animal symbol, you are neat, smart, and vigilant. You have potential to do great things by taking a leadership role. Please cultivate your patience, as it will help you to achieve your goals.

If Monkey is your monthly animal symbol, you have pretty good fortune in your life. Your health situation is good. Your great compassion and talent will help you to achieve your goal. Your life will be richer as time passes.

If Monkey is your hourly animal symbol, you are sympathetic, smart, and loveable. You have an unstable life when you are young. But you have a great life after these rough times. You might feel some difficulties around your relationship with your parents and siblings. It is a wise choice to live away from your parents. However, you have a great marriage. You and your partner will live happily and harmoniously together for a long time. Make sure to take good care of yourself and practice some inner cultivation when you are 19, 22, 26, 38, 49, and 77 years old. During these years, you have potential susceptibilities for sickness or accidents. Inner cultivation will help you smooth these years.

Monkey Landscape (Break, Simplify your Life)

Autumn water, a
changing beauty

Colorful leaves, her
instant fashion

Life reality, a dream pattern

Wisdom Sword, break
through Illusion

I will categorize some general Monkey features here for your further interest.

Personality

You are intelligent, attentive, spontaneous, smart, elegant, and wise. It is also common for Monkey people to be opportunistic, silly, or rushed. As a Monkey animal person, you have nimble wits and wisdom, which will help you to achieve your goals. Your flexible and attentive nature will help you to achieve your dreams. Sometimes, you might be hurried to get things done, so it is wise to cultivate your patience.

Health

You have good health potential. It might weaken your circulation and immune systems if you suffer some grief energy in your life. Finding the joy in your life will keep you in good shape.

Relationships

A Snake, Rat, or Dragon person may be your soul mate, or at least can be your very close friend. A Rooster or Dog person will make a great business partner for you. Be careful around a Pig person because it is easy to have some conflicts between the two of you. Try to make peace with a Tiger person – sometimes, you may get into fights for no real reason. You will have simple relationships with other animal symbol people.

Career

With your intelligent and wise character, you are well suited as a director, contractor, teacher, designer, or leader in the community.

Finance

You have ability to make money and are good at managing money. You have a rich life in general.

Color

White is your spirit's original color, and will always help you feel deeply connected with your spirit. Black is the color that will help you find your own potential energy and talent. Dressing in black when you have an important social activity, such as public speaking or lecturing, will help to accentuate your talent. Red will help you feel grounded. As green is your financial color, it will bring you good luck in your finances – so have some green in your office! Yellow or brown are your spiritual source colors and having them in your cultivation room or bedroom will nourish your body physically and spiritually.

Food

Red color vegetables, oatmeal, pungent spices (like garlic and onion), fish, and nuts are good for you.

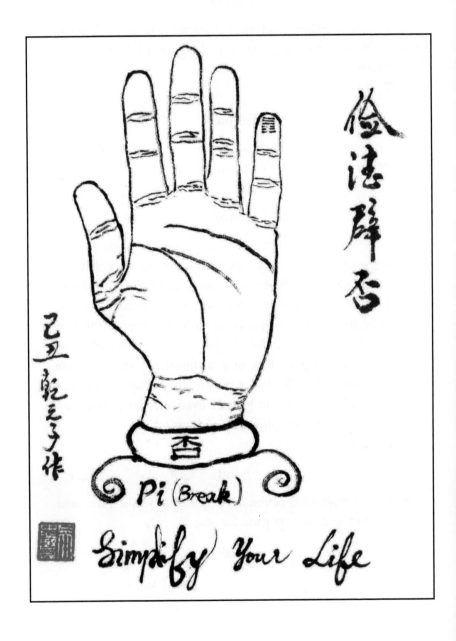

否

Pi (Break)

Simplify Your Life

Pi (Break)

Pi is the tidal hexagram that represents the energetic pattern of the Monkey animal symbol. The Chinese character *Pi* means deny, block, negate, misfortune, extinct, and break. The symbol of the hexagram is made with three *Yin* lines at the bottom and three *Yang* lines on top. This symbol represents *Yang Qi*, or life energy, getting weaker than the previous pattern *Dun*, in a natural cycle. The combination of three *Yin* lines and three *Yang* lines within the hexagram indicates that *Yin* and *Yang* energies are breaking in to their equal stage. *Pi* represents the time or place where you need to break through the old pattern and prepare a new strategy for the future.

In an annual cycle, *Pi* represents the *Shen* month, which occurs from approximately August 8 to September 8 in a solar calendar. This is the first month of the autumn season according to Chinese cosmology. It is also the time that plants are completely ripened and ready for the harvest in the northern hemisphere. *Shen* symbolizes holding your energy deep within, just as it is the time when trees begin to withdraw their life energy back to the roots, allowing the leaves to start changing color, and preparing to let them go. *Shen* also represents the wisdom of stepping back from your old position and releasing attachments when it is necessary.

In a daily cycle, *Pi* stands for *Shen* time, which is 15:00–16:59. This time period is comparable to the first month in autumn, when nature is turning to its golden color. This is the time that you should hold your activity back and make space for the coming changes in the next stage of your life. In general, it is the best time for getting your old things done without attachment.

Let us discover more information about *Pi* from *Yijing* wisdom. The hexagram *Pi* is made up of two trigrams: the top trigram is *Qian* (Heaven) and the bottom trigram is *Kun* (Earth). It is an image of Heaven over Earth. Heaven is the symbol for circulating and strengthening new life energy or power. Earth has the quality of openness, greatness, and carrying everything. Like the mother, the Earth does not show off, yet it holds, carries, and supports all beings. The hexagram *Pi* is a pattern of the disconnection between Heaven and Earth: the Heavenly *Qi* stays above and Earthly *Qi* stays below, which shows the killing power of nature. *Pi* is an image of your inner cultivation: when you feel difficulties in your life or frustration with your inner cultivation, it is time for you to break the old patterns you have, and to make conscious decisions to detach from anything that no longer serves you. Detachment does not mean disconnection. Like the autumn season, nature lets its old life pattern go – trees allow their leaves to change their color and fall down, but they hold their true life energy deep within their roots, cultivating it for the next new life pattern in the spring.

The wisdom of the hexagram *Pi* (Break) advises us that we should let go of our old patterns of life or spiritual cultivation when it is necessary. Detachment is an important way to uplift your spirit. This same principle applies to health as well. When you get sick or have a block in your life, it is often the best time for you to change your old lifestyle habits. There is a peaceful and harmonious way of life waiting for you. I hope you can try some inner cultivation with me at *Pi* time; it is a time for you to break old patterns in your life and to completely awaken your inner power and wisdom.

Inner Cultivation *Pi* ceremony

At any time when you need help improving your quality of life, or when you are experiencing hard times, light a candle in front of you and start this meditation.

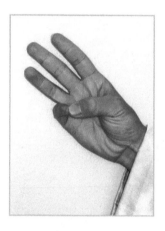

First straighten your back and feel that your body is stable like a mountain. Then, make the *Pi* mudra by placing each thumb on the tip of the little finger. The tip of the little finger is related to the hexagram *Pi*. Opening and relaxing your fingers, please place your right palm by your lower belly (close to your navel), facing earth, and place your left palm above your head, facing heaven. Adjust your breathing to be slow, smooth, deep, and even. Feel each breath connecting with your stomach, large intestines, and bladder. Meditate as long as you can. Before ending, please say a little prayer:

*"May the Spiritual Lights shine on
my pure spiritual body,*

*May the Spiritual Lights shine on
my golden sword of wisdom,*

*May the Spiritual Lights shine on
my path of eternal life."*

10

Rooster and
Guan 觀
(Observe)

觀天下之神道而四時不忒
乙酉雞
感

The rooster has beautiful feathers, strong claws, and an elegant crown. Roosters give you a classy and calm feeling when they are quiet. But, once they get into a fight, they are brave and powerful. They crow every morning at the same time. In the Chinese tradition, Rooster is a symbol for faith, attractiveness, power, affection, and nobility. It is the tenth animal symbol in the 12 Chinese Animals System. We use *You* 酉 to represent the Rooster symbol in the 12 Earthly Branches. *You* is a symbol for the 17:00–18:59 time of day, and for the eighth month in the Chinese Lunar-Solar calendar, which is approximately September 8 to October 8 in the Gregorian solar calendar. *You* represents the sunset time of day and the harvest month of the year. It is a time or a place where *Yang* energy (life energy) is declining, moving into its retired stage in a life cycle. We use the tidal hexagram *Guan* to symbolize Rooster.

Having a Rooster animal symbol in your Chinese birth chart suggests you are stylish, intelligent, influential, and faithful, and have a sense of humor; you can sometimes be arrogant, or proud. You have great intuition, which will help you to foresee your future direction clearly. You are good at making a schedule. Your natural prescient ability will allow you to complete your tasks perfectly.

People love your influential and intuitive nature. You will do well to choose a managerial job, such as a manager, organizer, inventor, developer, advisor, or lecturer. When you work directly with people, please remember to slow down your speech because people might feel that it is difficult to keep up with you. The important thing for you to keep in mind if you are in a relationship is to learn how to communicate with your partner gently.

If Rooster is your yearly animal symbol, you will likely have a lovely life. Your intelligence and responsibility will make your business successful. You should cultivate your flexibility and softness which will help make your life easier, with less conflict.

If Rooster is your monthly animal symbol, you have great humanity, wisdom, and justice. You have great artistic and literary potential. You will have a great life.

If Rooster is your hourly animal symbol, you have a big heart to help others. You have a wobbly life when you are young. You will feel more comfortable about your life after 50 and you will enjoy your retirement life. Make sure to take good care of yourself when you are 22, 28, 39, 46, and 77. During these years, it is possible you may get into some trouble.

Rooster Landscape (Observe, Discover the Way of Nature)

Sun is getting his rest

Sky is lasting in twilight

Moon is revealing her mystery

God within you watching all

I will categorize some general Rooster features here for your further interest.

Personality

You are stylish, intelligent, influential, faithful, and have a sense of humor; you can sometimes be arrogant, or proud. Your great intuition and natural prescient ability will allow you to complete your tasks perfectly, often with an intriguing element of surprise! Cultivating your flexibility will help you to work through difficult times with ease and achieve your greatest goals in life.

Health

Generally speaking, you have pretty good health. You have a potential weakness in your lungs, so please practice daily breathing exercises to keep you sharp.

Relationships

A Snake, Ox, or Dragon person may be your soul mate, or at least can be your very close friend. A Monkey person will make a great business partner for you. Be aware of a Dog person: while it is easy to attract each other, there are some conflicts between you two. Try to make peace with a Rabbit person – sometimes, you may get into fights for no real reason. You will have simple relationships with other animal symbol people.

Career

With your charming and natural insight, you are well suited as a manager, organizer, inventor, developer, advisor, or lecturer.

Finance

You do not have trouble with money. Money will come to you if you keep doing great things for others.

Color

White is your spirit's original color, and will always help you to feel deeply connected with your spirit. Black is the color that will help you to find your own potential energy and talent. Dressing in black when you have an important social activity, such as public speaking or lecturing, will help to accentuate your talents. Red will help you to feel grounded. As green is your financial color, it will bring you good luck in your finances – so have some green in your office! Yellow or brown are your spiritual source colors, and having them in your cultivation room or bedroom will nourish your body physically and spiritually.

Food

Green vegetables, fermented foods, oatmeal, pungent spices (like garlic and onion), fish, black beans, chrysanthemum tea, and nuts are good for you.

萬物靜觀

觀
Guan (observe)

Discover the Way of Nature

Guan (Observe)

Guan is the tidal hexagram that represents the energetic pattern of the Rooster animal symbol. The Chinese character *Guan* means display, visit, watch, advise, and observe. The symbol of the hexagram is made with four *Yin* lines at the bottom and two *Yang* lines on top. This symbol represents *Yang Qi*, or life energy, getting weaker than the previous pattern *Pi*, in a natural cycle. The symbolic meaning of *Guan* represents the time or place to simply watch to see what is going on, having no need to struggle.

In an annual cycle, *Guan* represents the *You* month, which occurs from approximately September 8 to October 8 in a solar calendar. This is the second month of the autumn season according to Chinese cosmology. It is also the time that the weather is cooling and nature is changing to its golden color in most areas in the northern hemisphere. This is the time when farmers harvest their land. *You* symbolizes retiring and enjoying time with family and nature when the time is right.

ZhongQiu 中秋, the Mid-Autumn Festival, is one of the most important festivals in Chinese tradition. *ZhongQui* occurs on the full moon of this month. The moon on this night is considered to be the brightest and fullest moon of the year. This is the brightest time in the whole year, according to Chinese tradition. In traditional agrarian communities, people would join together to celebrate the harvest and to relax and enjoy time with family and friends. Even in modern times, people still follow the tradition of *ZhongQiu* of reuniting to savor the autumn harvest. In China, the full moon represents harmony, reunion, and nature completing its full circle. Imagine we live far away and cannot see one another or have the chance to meet to celebrate this special day. If we lift our heads and watch the full moon, our energy will always connect. It is said we can feel this connection more deeply through this special moon. In ancient times, it was difficult for people who lived far away from one another to get together, or even to communicate with one another, so they would simply gaze at the full moon to feel the connection with family and friends.

In a daily cycle, *Guan* stands for *You* time, which is 17:00–18:59. This time period is comparable to the second month in autumn. This is the time that you should be action-less and enjoy yourself. It is one of the best cultivation times for you to settle down your life energy and transform it into a high conscious state.

Let us discover more information about *Guan* from *Yijing* wisdom. The hexagram *Guan* is made up of two trigrams: the top trigram is *Xun* (Wind) and the bottom trigram is *Kun* (Earth). It is an image of Wind on the Earth. *Xun* is a symbol for vitality and life energy, and strong momentum. The attribute of *Xun* is the ability to proceed and to propagate in a gentle manner. Earth has the quality of openness, greatness, and carrying everything. Like the mother, the Earth does not show off, yet it holds, carries, and supports all beings. The hexagram *Guan* is an image of autumn wind blowing off the leaves and the old weak branches of trees, making nature clear. *Guan* is also the image of you in meditation: you hold your posture stable like the Earth, regulating your breath like a powerful wind, so that you can easily bring your eyesight and mind within to completely awaken your physical and spiritual body.

The wisdom of the hexagram *Guan* (Observe) advises that when we are in chaotic or unpredictable circumstances, it is wise to step back and just watch to learn the situation clearly. Your daily cultivation will help you to maintain well-being and make decisions about your future direction with certainty. I hope you can try some inner cultivation with me at *Guan* time; it is a time for you to slow down and scrutinize your life.

Inner Cultivation *Guan* ceremony

At any time when you need help making a new decision, or you would like to take care of yourself, light a candle in front of you and start this meditation.

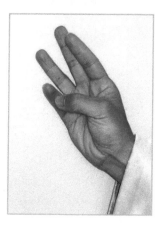

First straighten your back and feel that your body is stable like a mountain. Then, make the *Guan* mudra by placing each thumb on the top crease of the little finger. The top crease of the little finger is related to the hexagram *Guan*. Opening and relaxing your fingers, encircle your arms in front of you with your palms facing your chest. Adjust your breathing to be slow, smooth, deep, and even. Feel each breath connecting with your lungs and with your whole body. Meditate as long as you can. Before ending, please say a little prayer:

"*May the Spiritual Lights completely
awaken my physical body,*

*May the Spiritual Lights completely
awaken my energetic body,*

*May the Spiritual Lights completely
awaken my spiritual body.*"

11

Dog and *Bo* 剥 (Peel)

戌狗
剝順而
止之天
行也

Dog is the closest friend of human beings. Dog helps human beings to hunt, investigate, and guard. Dog is a symbol of bravery, caution, honesty, and loyalty. Dog is the eleventh animal symbol in the 12 Chinese Animals System. We use *Xu* 戌 to represent the Dog symbol in the 12 Earthly Branches. *Xu* is a symbol for the 19:00–20:59 time of day, and for the ninth month in the Chinese Lunar-Solar calendar, which is approximately October 8 to November 7 in the Gregorian solar calendar. *Xu* represents the supper time of day, and the third autumn month when nature is ready for the winter season. It is a time or a place where *Yang* energy (life energy) is in further decline and close to its end of the life cycle. We use the tidal hexagram *Bo* to symbolize Dog.

Having a Dog animal symbol in your Chinese birth chart suggests you are intuitive, smart, artistic, cautious, social, honest, and loyal, and can sometimes be uneasy, evasive, or stubborn. You have a truthful and creative nature, which will help you to achieve your goals. You have a tendency to be overconfident in your own judgment, and sometimes you may not want to listen to other people. It will be helpful when completing your tasks if you can consider other people's opinions before you take a new step in your life.

You would do well to choose a job that requires artistic effort, such as a musician, painter, calligrapher, art designer, film maker, doctor, or healer. When you work directly with people, you would be wise to continually cultivate your gentleness, otherwise, you may come across as being headstrong. The most important thing for you to remember if you are going to have a relationship is to ask for a second opinion from a trusted friend.

If Dog is your yearly animal symbol, you have great talent and will probably have a pretty stable life. You are likely to achieve your goals before you are 35 years old. You will need to work doubly hard to make a successful project after you are 35 years old.

If Dog is your monthly animal symbol, you have a strong, tough personality, which might cause some trouble in your life. However, you will have a great, successful life if you can cultivate your gentleness and virtue.

If Dog is your hourly animal symbol, you are handsome, beautiful, and talented and you have a joyful life. You might experience the sorrow of losing your family in the late stage of your life. Make sure to take good care of yourself and have nice vacations when you are 14, 26, 29, and 36 years old. Be very careful when you are 75 years old because you might have a major health problem at this time.

Dog Landscape (Peel, Let it Go)

Mountain stands on Earth steadily
Wind rain dissolves it gently
Sun-moon shuttles
endless time river
Ruin retains no constant matter

I will categorize some general Dog features here for your further interest.

Personality

You are intuitive, smart, artistic, cautious, social, honest, and loyal, and can sometimes be uneasy, evasive, or stubborn. Your truthful and creative nature will help you to complete your tasks and achieve your greatest goals in life.

Health

In general, you have a pretty healthy life. Please give yourself at least a half-hour exercise time every day. Otherwise, you may have minor health issues related to your digestion. Eat well and sleep well to avoid having concerns about your digestion, heart, and lung health.

Relationships

A Tiger, Rabbit, or Horse person may be your soul mate, or at least can be your very close friend. A Monkey person will make a great business partner for you. Be careful around a Rooster person because it is easy to have some conflicts between you two, even though both of you may sometimes feel as close as siblings. Try to make peace with a Dragon person – sometimes, you may get into fights for no real reason. You will have simple relationships with other animal symbol people.

Career

With your intuitive and artistic nature, you can be well suited as a musician, painter, calligrapher, art designer, film maker, doctor, or healer.

Finance

You can have a pretty comfortable life without worrying about finances. In general, winter is a good season for you to increase your financial power.

Color

Yellow or brown are your spirit's original colors, and they will always help you feel deeply connected with your spirit. White is the color that will help you to find your own potential energy and talent. You should wear white clothes when you have an important social activity, such as public speaking or lecturing. Green will help you feel grounded. As black is your financial color, it will bring you good luck in your finances to have some black in your office. Red is your spiritual source color, and having it in your cultivation room or bedroom will nourish your body physically and spiritually.

Food

Root vegetables, black beans, fermented foods, pungent and bitter spices, and fish are good for you.

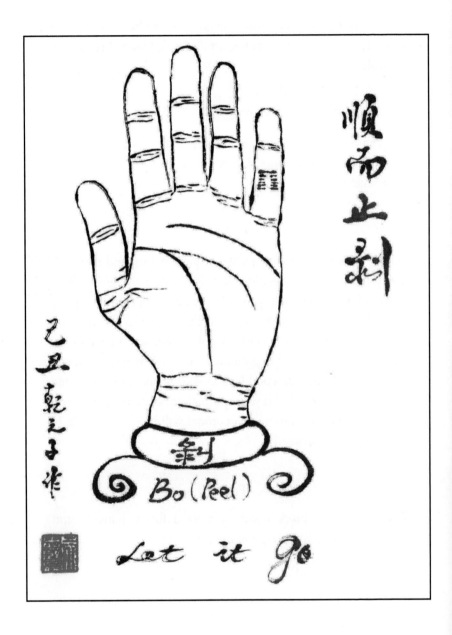

順而止剝

乙丑乾元子作

剝
Bo (Peel)

Let it go

Bo (Peel)

Bo is the tidal hexagram that represents the energetic pattern of the Dog animal symbol. The Chinese character *Bo* means tear off, fall off, decorticate, and peel. The symbol of the hexagram is made with five *Yin* lines on the bottom and one *Yang* line on top. This symbol represents *Yang Qi*, or life energy, declining further than the previous pattern *Guan*, in a natural cycle. It represents the time or place where you should let all the old patterns of your life go. *Bo* represents the wisdom of holding yourself stable no matter what dramatic thing is happening in your life.

In an annual cycle, *Bo* represents the *Xu* month, which occurs from approximately October 8 to November 7 in a solar calendar. This is the last month of the autumn season according to Chinese cosmology. It is also the time when nature is getting its final preparations for the winter season in the northern hemisphere. It is the end of the season of change.

Change is not easy, because it involves "letting it go." The process of change and letting go is exemplified in nature this month; leaves have changed their colors and fallen off the branches, fruits have dropped from trees – the old patterns of nature are coming to an end. In our lives, we may want to make the changes but can be afraid to do so because we hold many old patterns in our minds. Our lives would feel more peaceful and harmonious if we would always remember to breathe deeply into the Dantian no matter what happens in our lives and in the world. When we can't change the external circumstances of our lives, we can change our minds, attitudes, and spirits to make our future brighter.

In a daily cycle, *Bo* stands for *Xu* time, which is 19:00–20:59. This time period is comparable to the last month in autumn, when nature has reached its greatest peeling – deciduous plants lose all their leaves and drop their fruits. This is the time to meditate on letting go of your old life patterns, to prepare for your next life stage.

Let us discover more information about *Bo* from *Yijing* wisdom. The hexagram *Bo* is made up of two trigrams: the top trigram is *Gen* (Mountain) and the bottom trigram is *Kun* (Earth). It is an image of a mountain lying on the Earth. A mountain represents the stability and spiritual quality of the trigram *Gen*. It indicates that in our daily life, we need to have internal stability, just like a mountain. *Kun* stands for the nature spirits that are hidden within the Earth. Earth does not show off, yet it holds, carries, and supports all beings. Combined, the hexagram *Bo* becomes an image of a great stableness of nature – trees peel off their leaves and sick branches and hold their life energy deep within the roots, migrating birds shed their weak feathers to make their wings stronger for the next journey, animals hold their energy within to prepare for the winter. Through these changes, nature holds the life stable for the next spring season or new life cycle. *Bo* is also the image of you in meditation: when you hold your back and body steady for a long time period, you can easily feel the changes happening in your body, you can feel yourself becoming more grounded and effortlessly connect with your inner peace.

The wisdom of the hexagram *Bo* (Peel) advises us that we should let go of old life patterns once change has begun. Instead of resisting the change, this is the time to be solid, stable, and action-less. Accept the change and let it go. I hope you can try some inner cultivation with me at *Bo* time; it is a time for you to look deep within and listen deep within, allowing great transformation to take place.

Inner Cultivation *Bo* ceremony

At any time when you need help being centered, or you are facing a dramatic shift in your life, light a candle in front of you and start this meditation.

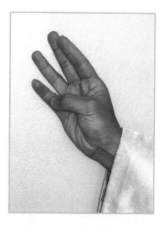

First straighten your back and feel that your body is stable like a mountain. Then, make the *Bo* mudra by placing each thumb on the second crease of the little finger. The second crease of your little finger is related to the hexagram *Bo*. Opening and relaxing your fingers, encircle your arms with palms facing your lower belly. Adjust your breathing to be slow, smooth, deep, and even. Feel each breath connecting with your stomach, heart, and lungs. Meditate as long as you can. Before ending, please say a little prayer:

*"May the Spiritual Lights completely
awaken the root of my life,*

*May the Spiritual Lights completely
awaken the root of my breath,*

*May the Spiritual Lights completely awaken
the root of my consciousness."*

12

Pig and *Kun* 坤 (Flow)

Pigs enjoy their food and their sleep. The pig gives us a relaxing or even a lazy feeling. The pig is actually a very intelligent animal. In the Chinese tradition, Pig is a symbol of relaxation, caution, braveness, knowledge, and faith. It is the twelfth animal symbol in the 12 Chinese Animals System. We use *Hai* 亥 to represent the Pig symbol in the 12 Earthly Branches. *Hai* is a symbol for the 21:00–22:59 time of day, and for the tenth month in the Chinese Lunar-Solar calendar, which is approximately November 7 to December 7 in the Gregorian solar calendar. In the daily cycle, *Hai* represents bed time, the time to take a deep rest both physically and mentally, and the first month of winter in the annual cycle. It can represent either a time or a place in which *Yang* energy (life energy) is ending in a life cycle. We use the tidal hexagram *Kun* to symbolize Pig.

Having a Pig animal symbol in your Chinese birth chart suggests that you are gentle, knowledgeable, joyful, smart, honest, trustworthy, and brave. It is also common for Pig people to be angry or insecure. As a Pig animal person, your tenderness and knowledge will help you to achieve your goals. Due to a tendency to give up easily when experiencing difficulties, it can be challenging to get your projects done. You would be wise to cultivate your patience and endurance to help you reach your dreams.

Generally speaking, you have a pleasurable life. People like your intellect and leadership. You would do well to choose an influential job, like being a director, contractor, teacher, designer, or accountant. When you work directly with people, remember to continually cultivate your patience and self-confidence; otherwise, you may come across as being irritable or tough. The important thing for you to remember if you are in a relationship is to learn how to communicate with your partner with an open heart.

If Pig is your yearly animal symbol, you are neat, smart, kind, and reliable. You have potential to do great things by helping others. People admire your compassion and your leadership. Please cultivate your persistence and ability to share yourself, as it will help you to achieve your goals.

If Pig is your monthly animal symbol, you have very good fortune in your life. Your health situation is good. Your great compassion for others will help you achieve your goals. Your life will be great if you dedicate yourself to continuously helping others.

If Pig is your hourly animal symbol, you are diligent, direct, and kind. You have a challenging life when you are young, which eases nicely after those rough times. Make sure you take good care of yourself and practice some inner cultivation when you are 26, 36, 49, 56, and 88 years old. During these years, you have potential susceptibilities for sickness or accidents. Inner cultivation will help you to smooth these years.

Pig Landscape (Flow, Cultivate Great Virtue)

Mother Earth holds thick virtue
Vast land carries our future
Golden grass covers her feature
Flowing water nourishes
all creatures

I will categorize some general Pig features here for your further interest.

Personality

You are gentle, knowledgeable, joyful, smart, honest, trustworthy, and brave. It is also common for Pig people to be angry or insecure. As a Pig animal person, you have tenderness and knowledge, which will help you to achieve your goals. Your compassionate nature will help you to achieve your dreams. As you will have to overcome some difficulties in your life, it is wise to cultivate your endurance.

Health

You have great health potential. It might weaken your heart function if you overwork every day.

Relationships

A Tiger, Rabbit, or Goat person may be your soul mate, or at least can be your very close friend. A Rat or Ox person will make a great business partner for you. Be careful around a Monkey person because it is easy to have some conflicts between the two of you. Try to make peace with a Snake person – sometimes, you may get into fights for no real reason. You will have simple relationships with other animal symbol people.

Career

With your leadership and wise character, you may be well suited as a director, contractor, teacher, designer, or accountant.

Finance

You have good luck with money. You have a wealthy life in general.

Color

Black is your spirit's original color, and will always help you feel deeply connected with your spirit. Green is the color that will help you find your own potential energy and talent. Dressing in green when you have an important social activity, such as public speaking or lecturing, will help to accentuate your talents. Yellow or brown colors will help you feel grounded. As red is your financial color, it will bring you good luck in your finances – so have some red in your office! White is your spiritual source color, and having it in your cultivation room or bedroom will nourish your body physically and spiritually.

Food

Root vegetables, black color foods, lamb, fish, and nuts are good for you.

坤

Kun (Flow)

Cultivate Great Virtue

Kun (Flow)

Kun is the tidal hexagram that represents the energetic pattern of the Pig animal symbol. The Chinese character *Kun* means great, feminine, open, straight, mother, and flow. The symbol of the hexagram is made with three *Yin* lines at the bottom and three *Yin* lines on top. This symbol represents *Yang Qi*, or life energy, getting weaker than the previous pattern *Bo*, and reaching its lowest level in a natural cycle. The combination of six *Yin* lines within the hexagram indicates that *Yin* energies are dominating. *Kun* represents the time or place where you need to completely surrender yourself and follow the flow of nature.

In an annual cycle, *Kun* represents the *Hai* month, which occurs from approximately November 7 to December 7 in a solar calendar. This is the first month of the winter season according to Chinese cosmology. It is also the time that plants are completely holding their life energy back in their roots, and when animals are starting to hibernate in the northern hemisphere. *Hai* symbolizes holding your energy deeply within, just like the trees withdraw their life energy back to the roots in winter. *Hai* also represents the wisdom of hiding your talent and power when the situation does not support you.

In a daily cycle, *Kun* stands for *Hai* time, which is 21:00–22:59. This time period is comparable to the first month in winter, when nature is hibernating. This is the time that you should totally hold your activity back and make space for the new life energy or power returning in your next life cycle. In general, it is the best time for relaxing and going to sleep.

Let us discover more information about *Kun* from *Yijing* wisdom. The hexagram *Kun* is made up of two similar trigrams: the top trigram is *Kun* (Earth) and the bottom trigram is *Kun* (Earth). It is an image of Earth over Earth. Earth has the quality of openness, greatness, and carrying everything. Like the mother, the Earth does not show off, yet it holds, carries, and supports all beings. The six broken lines of the hexagram *Kun* is a pattern of the great virtue of Earth, showing the gentleness, openness, tenderness, and nature's power to give birth. *Kun* also teaches us that as Earth is part of the Heaven (Universe), the Earthly way follows the Heavenly way, yet the spirit of Heaven is hidden within the Earth. Therefore, *Kun* is an image of your inner cultivation: if you want to reach your highest spiritual state, you must be grounded, breathe into your Earth (lower belly), and cultivate your great virtue.

The wisdom of the hexagram *Kun* (Flow) advises us that great harmony arises from the free flowing *Qi* (Energy), which requires us to have the quality of *Kun* — softness, openness, stableness, and compassion. These same qualities will also bring you great health. Free flowing *Qi* is the source of a peaceful and harmonious way of life. I hope you can try some inner cultivation with me at *Kun* time; it is a time for you to be soft, gentle, and compassionate, to completely awaken your inner power and new life energy.

Inner Cultivation *Kun* ceremony

At any time when you need help awakening your inner power, or when you are seeking a new way of life, light a candle in front of you and start this meditation.

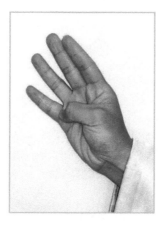

First straighten your back and feel that your body is stable like a mountain. Then, make the *Kun* mudra by placing each thumb on the base crease of the little finger. The base crease of the little finger is related to the hexagram *Kun*. Opening and relaxing your fingers, interlock your fingers and place your palms on your lower belly (right under your navel). Adjust your breathing to be slow, smooth, deep, and even. Feel each breath connecting with your gallbladder and urinary bladder. Meditate as long as you can. Before ending, please say a little prayer:

*"May the Spiritual Lights completely
awaken my great gentleness,*

*May the Spiritual Lights completely
awaken my great openness,*

*May the Spiritual Lights completely
awaken my great compassion."*

AFTERWORD

Living in Harmony

Life is precious! As I finish my writing on this book, I find I have gained a deeper understanding about the beauty of life, a central concept in Chinese wisdom traditions. In Chinese, we have a proverb – a living beggar is much nobler than a dead emperor. A living person, no matter what their station in life, is treasured because they are full of life. Ancient illuminated beings have passed down many teachings to us about how to respect and protect all beings by living in harmony with them, with ourselves, and with nature.

In Chinese, the word for harmony is *He* 和. The quality of *He* is expressed by the classical Chinese musical instrument, the *Qin* 琴, and the music it creates. A harmonious song has a resonance that will bring human beings and nature into a harmonious state. A great musician is able to channel the Universal *Qi* 气 (Energy) during a performance, which then affects the surrounding environment. *Yueshu* 乐书 (*The Book of Music*) tells us "No law is necessary if a ruler understands how to use harmonious music to rule the country." Harmony is the inexhaustible source of universal peace.

The function of Dao 道, or the Great Way of Nature, is to create harmony. In inner cultivation, we use the musical instrument *Qin* as the symbol for heart. By tuning your *Qin* (Heart) and following the Dao, you can be in command of the destiny of your life, living harmoniously, rather than succumbing to a fate of suffering. A central Daoist concept is that life is not controlled by fate or karma alone – *wo ming zai wo bu zai tian* (我命在我不在天), or "my life is in my hand, and is not controlled by fate." Through mindfulness and effort, we all have the ability to achieve true autonomy. I hope this book will guide you to keep tuning your *Qin*, your own heart, to a peaceful state.

Living in harmony,

Zhongxian Wu
December 2009

About the Author

Master Zhongxian Wu was born on China's eastern shore in the city of Wenling in Zhejiang Province, where the sun's rays first touch the Chinese mainland. He began practicing Qigong and Taiji at an early age. Inspired by the immediate strengthening effects of this practice, Master Wu committed himself to the life-long pursuit of the ancient arts of internal cultivation. Over the next thirty years he devoted himself to the study of Qigong, martial arts, Chinese medicine, Yijing science, Chinese calligraphy, and ancient Chinese music, studying with some of the best teachers in these fields.

China's traditional arts and disciplines continue to be passed on within the time-honored discipleship system, wherein the acknowledged master of a given discipline instructs a close-knit circle of chosen students. Near the end of the master's life, the master selects the next "lineage holder" who will be responsible for the preservation of the entire system of knowledge. Master Wu is the lineage holder of four different schools of Qigong and martial arts:

- 18th generation lineage holder of the Mt. Wudang Dragon Gate style of Qigong (Wudang Longmen Pai)

- 8th generation lineage holder of the Mt. Emei Sage/ Shaman style Qigong (Emei Zhengong)

- 7th generation lineage holder of the Dai Family Heart Method style of Xin Yi (Dai Shi Xinyi Quan)

- 12th generation lineage holder of the Wudang He style of Taijiquan.

In China, Master Wu served as Director of the Shaanxi Province Association for Somatic Science and the Shaanxi Association for the Research of Daoist Nourishing Life Practices. In this capacity, he conducted many investigations into the clinical efficacy of Qigong and authored numerous works on the philosophical and historical foundations of China's ancient life sciences.

In 2001, Master Wu left his job as an aerospace engineer in Xi'an, China, to teach in the United States. For four years he served as Senior Instructor and Resident Expert of Qigong and Taiji in the Classical Chinese Medicine Department at the National College of Naturopathic Medicine (NCNM) in Portland, Oregon. In addition to his work at NCNM, Master Wu was a sub-investigator in a 2003 Qigong research program sponsored by the National Institute of Health (NIH).

Since he began teaching in 1988, Master Wu has instructed thousands of Qigong students, both eastern and western. Master Wu is committed to bringing the authentic teachings of Chinese ancient wisdom tradition such as Qigong, Taiji, martial arts, calligraphy, Chinese astrology, and *Yijing* science to his students. He synthesizes wisdom and experience for beginning and advanced practitioners, as well as patients seeking healing, in his unique and professionally designed courses and workshops. Please visit www.masterwu.net for details about his teachings.

Master Wu has written six books and numerous articles on the philosophical and historical foundations of China's ancient life sciences, including the first Chinese Shamanic Qigong book in English, *Vital Breath of the Dao: Chinese Shamanic Tiger Qigong (Laohu Gong)*, also published by Singing Dragon.

Master Wu and his wife Karin currently reside in Virginia's Blue Ridge mountains where they founded Blue Willow Health Center (www.bluewillowhealthcenter.com).